Previous books by Zelda la Grange

Good Morning, Mr Mandela (2014)
Goeiemôre, Mnr. Mandela (2014)

What Nelson Mandela Taught Me

Timeless Lessons on Leadership and Life

Zelda la Grange

Tafelberg

Author's note: I have retained the name of the social media network Twitter, as that's what it was called at the time I refer to, before it was rebranded X.

Tafelberg,
an imprint of NB Publishers, a division of Media24 Boeke (Pty) Ltd
40 Heerengracht, Cape Town, South Africa
www.tafelberg.com

Quotations on pages 84, 128, 133, 146, 153, 181, 190 and 199 from *Nelson Mandela By Himself: The Authorised Book of Quotations* eds. Sello Hatang and Sahm Venter (South Africa: Pan Macmillan South Africa in association with Blackwell & Ruth, 2014) used by permission of the publisher.

Front cover photograph: Gallo Images/Reuters/Juda Ngwenya
Back cover photograph: Gallo Images/Foto24/Loanna Hoffmann
Cover and layout design: Marthie Steenkamp
Editing: Gillian Warren-Brown
Proofreading: Riaan Wolmarans and Janet Bartlet
Indexer: George Claassen

Set in Hermann Regular

First edition, first impression 2024

ISBN: 978-0-624-09550-7
Epub: 978-0-624-09551-4

Printed by **novus** *print*, a division of Novus Holdings

To every person who decides to change their own life, impact the lives of others, and defy a single-story narrative . . .

Contents

Contents

'Have you learnt nothing from Nelson Mandela?'

January 2015.

The red light on my mobile phone is flickering: eight missed calls. And about five times as many WhatsApp, email and text notifications. My first thought is: my parents. Are they okay? Only an emergency can be creating this amount of traffic on my phone.

It was an enormous adjustment after Madiba's passing not to guard my phone around the clock. As his personal aide, I wanted to always be available if he needed something or if anything happened to him. Now my priority has shifted to my own family.

I realise my phone is still on silent following my overnight flight to London. I should probably restore it to its normal setting, now that I have arrived in Oxford. I should also forward my calls to voicemail; it's so expensive to receive international roaming calls.

I guess the person who called so many times doesn't know that I simply hate telephone conversations. I spent nineteen years with a phone almost constantly glued to my ear while working for Nelson Mandela, fondly referred to by his Thembu clan name, Madiba. Enough phone time for a lifetime. In any case, can't the person hear from the ringtone that I'm abroad? My irritation morphs into concern when I look at the call log: the names of two of my best friends appear repeatedly. They both know I'm overseas. They both know I'm the text-not-call type. What's so urgent that they can't say it in a text?

At least there's one positive: I feel relieved that since it's them trying to reach me, it can't be about the welfare of my family. I remove the phone from the charger and sit on the crisp white linen of the bed. The phone rings again and I quickly kill the call.

I open WhatsApp. 'Zelda,' one message starts. This particular friendship is a close one and a safe space because, ideologically, we always align. I simply love him, his wife and family, and consider them truthful and authentic people – those who remain friends long after your expiry date. He's like a younger brother who can say anything to me, and familiar enough never to have to use my name as a salutation. It's strange that he is using my name; his message immediately sounds formal. 'What have you done?' I read on. 'Call me,' he says. 'Call me urgently.' At first, I resist. I haven't done anything, I think to myself, so why would I call you?

'I'm overseas, as you know,' I start, 'and I can't make calls from here.' Mobile calls are way too expensive and WhatsApp data calling isn't part of our lives yet. 'What's up?' I ask. While he's typing, I open the next WhatsApp message: 'Babe,' it says, 'are you okay?' What's she talking about? 'Yes, thanks. I've just arrived in Oxford and I'm going for the dress rehearsal in about an hour.' I guess she wants to know if my trip went well; she's always so caring. This friend is a wise young woman I've come to depend on for emotional support after Madiba's death. She's fifteen years younger than me, but she has a deep understanding of life way beyond her age. So sweet . . . and I shrug it off.

As I open my email, countless little envelope symbols pop up; my inbox is crowded. The folks over at the TEDx auditorium won't call if they need me, I think to myself. They'll email, so I'd better check if they need me earlier. Or perhaps there's a delay and they want me to stay at the hotel a little longer, in which case I may take a short nap. I am tired. Apart from the two long flights I took, it's also emotional exhaustion from being so angry earlier in the morning at the government squandering Madiba's legacy.

'Dear Zelda, we would like to do an interview with you,' the first email reads. That's great, I think, they want to talk to me about my upcoming TEDx talk at Oxford University. Then I continue reading the sentence: 'about your tweets this morning'. Oh, that. I brush it off as people simply wanting to create a story on a quiet Saturday morning when the news is slow. Why would they want to talk to me about my tweets? I open Twitter. I had written:

> 🐦 I'm sure comments like: it is un-African to have dogs, stress is a Western creation, Van Riebeeck etc all good for investment in SA.

> 🐦 The organisation that praises Mugabe but condemns [former president FW] De Klerk doesn't want us in SA.

> 🐦 Yes Mr De Klerk was the last apartheid president and gave in under pressure BUT he could have held onto power = civil war.

> 🐦 De Klerk surrendered power or he could have stayed in power like the other anarchists and corrupt heads of state around us.

> 🐦 If I was a white investor I would more or less leave now. It's very clear from Jacob Zuma whites are not wanted or needed in South Africa.

> 🐦 Oh wait. Whites' tax money is good enough for Nkandla but then you constantly have to be brutalised.

Soon after firing off this barrage, I had gone back online and sarcastically changed my profile name to Zelda van Riebeeck.

I go to my notifications page. Oh, at least this person agrees with me. Great, I think. And many people liked what I said. What's the problem?

I scroll down and start feeling the hate:

- 🐦 You bloody racist.

- 🐦 What did Mandela see in you?

- 🐦 You white c*nt.

- 🐦 We told you whites hate us. She is proof of that.

- 🐦 We knew Mandela sold out when he appointed a white woman.

- 🐦 Apartheid apologist.

- 🐦 F**king idiot.

- 🐦 If you are so unhappy, why don't you go back to Europe?

- 🐦 We don't want you here.

And so it continues. Only here and there some have tweeted their support of my sentiments. But the hatred is in free-fall.

Someone asks, 'Do you think Zelda's account was hacked?' Of course my account was not hacked. Sometimes, people who have tweeted garbage resort to claiming their account was hacked, to limit the damage. Mine was definitely not. I'm quite content with what I said.

My close friend calls again, and this time I answer.

'Do you realise that in your tweets you pretended that white suffering in South Africa took precedence over centuries of black suffering in our country?' he asks.

'No, that's not what I meant,' I reply.

'Yes, but that's how it appears, and Twitter is going crazy.'

'I saw that,' I mumble indignantly, 'but many people feel the same way I do, and I'm sick of Jacob Zuma using white people as an excuse for his inability to run the country. Why the blame game? Why always pick on the racial issues? Why is everything in this country about race?'

In that moment I had not considered that picking on white people was merely a tactic to distract and polarise South Africans. My assessment of the situation was wrong.

A few moments of silence follow. I don't know how to respond any further. I don't believe that what I tweeted was wrong. Instead, what goes through my mind is: how dare people take a particular meaning from something I didn't say?

It feels as if I've just been scolded by my favourite teacher. My friend's anger is clear, but more so his disappointment, even though I know it's motivated by deep care for my wellbeing.

At the time, I thought the worst thing that could happen to me was to disappoint anyone.

We end the call, concluding that we need to see where the conversation goes on Twitter before I do anything. Hopefully it'll die down soon.

I immediately go back onto Twitter. More likes, retweets and responses, and many more messages of encouragement, but equally so, insults and swearing as the engagement counter increases by the second.

I feel nauseous as I pour another cup of coffee. Maybe I'll feel better if I eat something. Perhaps I'm just 'hangry' – hungry-angry. I had breakfast on the plane at about 4 am; now it's almost noon. The thought of food makes me feel sick, though, and I quickly shift my thoughts.

Some of the comments are hurtful, some ridiculously obscene and others laughable. My head is spinning. How do I stop this train? I become aware of my racing heartbeat and realise that I'm in full-blown panic mode; my chest even feels tight.

I answer another call, this one from my young friend. 'I know your thoughts and feelings are valid,' she says, 'and remember no one can ever deny anyone feeling a particular emotion, but your choice of words and how you expressed yourself is perhaps where the problem started.'

'Well, what do I do now?' I ask.

'Let me think for a while,' she responds. We agree to speak again after the dress rehearsal for my TEDx talk, scheduled for the next day.

If others had called about something I'd said or done, I would have considered it their opinion and dealt with it in that way. But two of my closest friends calling me about the same issue obviously elevates it to another level, because of the huge level of respect I have for them.

I continue to read the responses to my tweets, and I feel hurt and disappointed. I'm still on the defence, but I mull over the two conversations I've just had.

I go into the trends section of Twitter and see that #Zelda is trending at number one. This scares me because I realise I'm trending not because of agreement but due to disagreement.

I read some of the retweets and opinions added by people I hold in high regard. Even they seem disappointed in me. To some I respond, but I dig the hole even deeper with every response I send. How did this go so wrong? People are all fed up with the president. Why am I not allowed to express my opinion without consequence?

I look up from the phone. The weak winter sun is shining into the hotel room. Suddenly I feel bitterly cold, despite having taken a long, hot shower. I'm obviously in shock. My breathing has become shallow. I have to fight back the tears. How did this happen?

I'd landed earlier that morning at London's Heathrow Airport on a connecting flight from Dubai. Throughout the night, news headlines from South Africa had appeared on the screen in front of me: President Jacob Zuma blames the country's current failures squarely on apartheid and colonialism.

I'd worked myself up about it and, feeling frustrated while standing in the long immigration queue at the airport, I'd taken out my phone, switched on the data and started tweeting.

14

I had no idea of the tsunami my hasty comments had unleashed back home until I scrolled through the stomach-churning vitriol hours later in my rather grand hotel in Oxford.

In my hotel room, the anger I felt earlier in the morning resurfaces. President Zuma blaming Jan van Riebeeck for the problems we face today is simply cheap politicking. He is trying to distract us from the absolute failure of the state to deliver on their promises of 21 years ago, I think as I brush my teeth for the third time that day. (You can never brush your teeth enough after being on an aeroplane for so long. I hope the feeling of fluff in my mouth is now gone.)

The clock is ticking, and I have to get ready for the rehearsal of my talk and still find my way to the theatre. I have no idea of directions; I'd planned to download them from Google Maps and navigate my way there on foot. After zipping up my boots, I pick up my phone again. More messages, outrage and questions. I switch on the kettle. I need another cup of coffee before I go out. My head spins.

Where is this bloody dress rehearsal? How the hell am I supposed to find it by myself? Completely misdirected anger, I quickly remind myself. I realise that this comes from my upbringing, and from the 1980s and 1990s in South Africa, when anger was such a big part of our existence. I know I still use anger as a defence.

I have to gather my things – handbag, hat, gloves and scarf – but I go round in circles in the small yet beautiful room, decorated Victorian-style. Compose yourself, I coach myself. You're about to stand on the biggest stage of your life to deliver a TEDx talk and you can't find your gloves. Ha. I realise my thoughts are becoming irrational. I'm too nervous. I'm going to mess up this talk because I'm so distracted. Never mind the biggest stage of my life; also the biggest embarrassment of my life. What if I get stage fright tomorrow and I can't go on stage? My mind races through different scenarios of complete failure. What if I forget the twelve-minute text I'm supposed to have memorised?

As I walk through the revolving door at the hotel entrance, I welcome the fresh, crisp air outside. It has a calming effect. It always strikes me when I travel abroad how hotel windows can hardly ever open. For a South African accustomed to fresh air even during our mild winters, this breeze is a welcome pick-me-up. It brings me back to reality. The sky is grey-blue without a cloud in sight, and the vastness makes me feel insignificant. I'm fighting back the tears as I try to compose myself.

People are going about their daily routine. This is supposedly the most beautiful university town in the world, but in this moment I struggle to notice anything beautiful. In my imagination, I'm in the gap between two trapezes and heading for a free-fall as I'm unable to grasp either swing: the TEDx talk ahead of me, and the Twitter storm brewing behind me.

As I look down at my boots treading on a pavement saturated with history and tradition, I feel like an imposter. I don't belong here, I think. There's nothing here for me. Why did I agree to do this? It'll most certainly be a disaster. People hate me. That's what they say on Twitter. I'm a disappointment. The thoughts keep rolling.

Somehow, I manage to find my way to the theatre. I try to be brave as I'm introduced to the organisers. I expect someone to say at any moment, 'Oh, we notice you're trending on Twitter. Would you mind sharing your thoughts on the accusation about racism?' or 'We think we need to remove you from tomorrow's bill.' I expect the worst. I try to be friendly, forcing a smile, but my voice is rough and cracked.

'You'll wait in this room,' one of the organisers says while showing me around backstage. My mind is back in South Africa, and I'm hardly registering all the instructions. What do I do? The words run in an endless loop through my mind. To my surprise, the organisers are friendly and courteous. They probably simply haven't seen it yet.

Suddenly, I'm on stage, blinded by the lights and standing on the white marker indicating the position I am supposed to take for the cameras during my speech. I feel small and even more inadequate than I anticipated. I want to cry, but I realise no one in the theatre would understand my emotion – they have no context and it would be inappropriate. There's silence until a man says over the loudspeaker, 'Sorry, Miss, did you hear me?'

My thoughts had gone back to the first time I met Madiba, when he told me I was 'overreacting' when I started crying. Meeting him, I'd felt a mixture of shock, guilt and a sense of being responsible for his incarceration. Now I recognise that same confusion – feeling guilty and ashamed at the same time. Yet again, I compose myself.

'I didn't quite hear what you said. Can you repeat, please?'

Calmly, he says, 'Would you like to run through your presentation now?'

'Oh, no no no, it's fine, thank you.' Right now, I cannot deliver my speech with conviction. I'm definitely not getting on this stage tomorrow, I think to myself. Absolutely not. I don't need a rehearsal because I'm not doing this talk. How can I stand here and talk while my entire world is imploding outside this theatre?

'Okay, then. We'll see you tomorrow,' the man answers, and the next speaker is called to the stage. I've failed, I think. I've already failed. I was invited to present at TEDx Oxford to share some of the lessons I'd learnt from Madiba over the nineteen years I'd worked for him. Also, in June 2014, six months before, my memoir, *Good Morning, Mr Mandela*, was published.

During the publication process, the significance of what happened to me had sunk in. I – an innocent, naive and unsophisticated young girl with brown eyes and two long braids – had really worked for Nelson Mandela for almost two decades. It was all over now and felt so far away but also as if it had all happened at once just yesterday.

The book was received positively, both in South Africa and abroad. Right from the start, I was clear that the book would not be a 'tell-all'. Despite this, I believed there was an expectation that it would reveal secrets and air dirty laundry. But there had been a covenant between

Madiba and me that I would never betray his trust – and it stands to this day.

In the weeks leading up to the launch of the book, Dr Makaziwe Mandela, Madiba's eldest daughter from his first marriage, issued a public threat to sue me for the publication of the book after parts of it were serialised in South Africa's Sunday newspapers. In response, I defended her right to do so. If there were any grounds for her to challenge the book, it was something I had to deal with, but I knew very well what a gruelling process I'd been subjected to during the legal checks. Once the editor had worked through the manuscript, several lawyers had gone through every sentence to ensure that confidentiality hadn't been breached and that there would be no grounds for defamation claims. I was asked questions such as: 'Is there someone who will stand up in court for you to support what you claim?' and 'Can you confirm that there is proof of this in any form?'

I'd made double sure, triple sure, that I was not in breach of any of the confidentiality conditions. It was more than a legal check for me; it was also about honouring a commitment.

I didn't expect the runaway success of the book and was blown away when the first print run sold out in South Africa in two days. A reprint followed almost immediately, and then, a few months later, two more. I certainly was not prepared for the success of the book internationally either. The Portuguese version was in the top 10 in Brazil, and it was received with equal enthusiasm in England, the US and France. It was translated into several languages, including Japanese and Chinese. But all this sounds like someone else's fairy tale. I simply try to get by every day; I still work to earn a living and I am saving to buy a new car, so the book clearly didn't earn me the millions of dollars that some suggested it did – and definitely not enough for me to retire on a tropical island!

I was surprised and felt humbled that my simple story could touch so many people. But more than anything, I was grateful that a South

African story had made it across the seas. I loved imagining that someone in a small village on the outskirts of the French Riviera would read my story in French, or that a commuter on a high-speed train in Japan would get to learn about our country in Japanese. I believe the book has helped readers to heal from the loss of one of the greatest and most beloved statesmen the world has ever known, and the end of an era. I hope it gave them insight into the human being behind the public persona of Nelson Mandela and that, perhaps for some, reading the book was a cathartic experience. Writing it certainly was. It gave me the chance to revisit memories and try to come to terms with what was a very personal loss. Perhaps I was also grieving for my purpose in life, which I'd felt had come to an end when Madiba died. The book gave me a new calling: to keep his legacy alive.

After my non-rehearsal, I rushed back to the hotel, oblivious of the route I'd taken to the theatre and back. The next day would bring the same challenge of trying to find my way. Of course, that was if I could persuade myself to go – a *very big* if at that point.

As I shut the door of my hotel room, my entire world caved in. I'd been rejected. I'd caused turmoil. I'd hurt people. I'd failed myself, but more importantly I'd failed Madiba. It was true: I was a disappointment. But how did I get there? In a question of minutes, the time it had taken for me to send that series of tweets, I'd lost focus.

I lay back on the bed and briefly admired the detail of the ornate moulded ceiling – until another thought muscled its way in: this was a colonial ceiling. Did I even like it? It was supposed to disgust me, like everything about colonialism.

Could the ceiling be beautiful, and the heavily draped curtains, the antique, exquisitely carved furniture and the silver tea set on the dresser? Could it remain beautiful when it was built on colonialism, which was so offensive and ugly? Madiba taught me to walk tall, to be aware of the past, but not for it to dictate my future or how I operated in the world. He made me and everyone else, no matter who or what we were, feel that we belonged. And now, that was gone. I didn't belong. Anywhere, for that matter, I thought.

I went back onto Twitter to try to understand the situation a little better, and to isolate where the ruckus had started. It was like scrolling through snapshots of my own funeral. Oh, at least that one is crying for me . . . Oh yes, I always knew you were just a hypocrite pretending to like me because you wanted something from me . . . and so every response illuminated more about the sender than I'd emotionally budgeted for.

It slowly dawned on me that my emotional outburst was completely out of line. If you truly understand the history of South Africa, you will realise that the burden of our colonial and apartheid past is very present in all of the socio-economic problems we face today. I realise that tweeting a number of ill-conceived lines on a messaging app, that only allows a certain amount of characters per tweet, was also the worst way to express myself. Although I have denounced apartheid publicly for the last twenty years, sending tweets in isolation, and from a place of anger and frustration, made it appear as if I praised apartheid and colonialism.

The journalist Eusebius McKaiser had sent a direct message (DM) after my second or third tweet earlier that morning. We'd communicated on Twitter, via DM, a few times but I'd never met him personally. I followed him on Twitter because his views were, at times, sobering. In this DM, he asked me what was happening and why I'd tweeted what I did. I responded that I was sick and tired of Zuma blaming apartheid and whites for all the problems in South Africa, calling journalist and commentator Max du Preez a racist and so forth. What I did not know was that Max and Eusebius had a history too. Eusebius took a screenshot of our private conversation and shared it on Twitter. My tweets had attracted some attention, but when Eusebius, with his many followers, shared that screenshot, it lit the kindling for a runaway fire.

As I read through the responses, it was like picking the scab off a half-healed wound, piece by piece. The blood was starting to ooze as the hatred surfaced, not only towards me but also among many people on Twitter.

Despite my shame, I registered that, lying there in a five-star hotel, I was so much better off than most black people in South Africa. In fact, better off than most people in South Africa. That couldn't be argued away.

I called my friend to talk things through.

We talked about people who did not pay income tax but did pay value-added tax and fuel levies through taxi fares and contributed financially in a host of other invisible ways. Just because a person didn't pay income tax, it didn't mean their tax money was worthless or that they didn't contribute to the economy. Even someone living below the poverty line paid tax, and their hardship after more than twenty years of broken government promises, and deterioration rather than progress, meant they had more reason to feel disappointment and anger at the government than I did.

After a long conversation, I finally understood how hurtful my comments had been to those black people who indeed believed in me and loved me. I'd denied them their experience by highlighting my so-called white suffering. They were ordinary people who only wanted to make South Africa work; people with no political aspirations and no hatred or grudges. I realised I had to apologise to these ordinary folks for creating the impression that white tax was more important than black tax. But I refused to apologise to Zuma. He was bankrupting our country and using us as a punchbag, and I did not want that to go unchallenged.

I thought, with some sadness, how far we'd moved away from the time when South Africans had a common purpose, when we'd felt that South Africa could, indeed, be a country where we could live in harmony and all would prosper. And so, with my friend, I started drafting an apology. I subsequently deleted the episode from my Twitter account, so what follows is a reconstruction from news outlets.

I began by apologising unconditionally to all South Africans who were offended by my tweets, adding, 'There is no "but" when hurting people who have nothing to do with your frustration.' I explained that I'd been out of the country for a week and, when I was catching up with local news, all the main news stories referred to whites, colonialism or apartheid. President Jacob Zuma was saying that all the country's problems had started when Jan van Riebeeck arrived in 1652. He was also calling Max du Preez a racist, and the African National Congress (ANC) was opposing a bid for a Cape Town street to be named after former president FW de Klerk. The headline about South Africa on my overnight flight had been 'South Africa in worst debt of 20 years: rand softens', with no article to explain.

In my apology, I confessed: 'I got angry. In an attempt to express my disdain at events, I failed to provide context and I was generalising.' I continued:

Colonisation was a terrible thing that happened to our country, but I cannot erase or change it . . . yet there are times when I feel it is regarded as the only wrong thing to have happened to this country. Yet we have a system that still wrongs people every day. Sorry if I have ruined your faith in me. Madiba was hardest on me, and my first apology should be to him for appearing to generalise. I am a proud South African Afrikaner wanting to build the future of our country. I cannot speak on anyone's behalf, but I can tell you how I feel. We are all frustrated and angry about the state of affairs. But that frustration is not limited to race or culture. All the racial blame game achieves is to distract from the real problems. These are corruption, mismanagement, inequality and the delivery of basic services. On any day our democracy is better than apartheid. But it does not mean we should not be critical of our state of affairs.

I read some of the comments and tried to respond and explain myself to certain people. But as time went on, the matter snowballed. Twitter users were now attacking each other. Conservative whites sided with me – the last thing I wanted – while others expressed their disapproval of my apology. The disapproval was becoming more toxic than the initial tweets. And people didn't read. At least 80 per cent of the anger vented over my apology implied that I'd apologised to Zuma, which I never did.

Half the country was angry at my tweets, and the other half was angry because I'd apologised. My tweets had divided people and I felt utterly ashamed that my ill-conceived emotional outburst, praising a colonial mastermind, had brought about anguish and pain. Once the cap that seals the bottle of intolerance is removed, it cannot be replaced. And I was the one who'd lifted that cap. People were telling me how disappointed they were in me, but that paled in comparison to how disappointed I was in myself.

Insults, threats to my safety and name calling followed. Group madness kicked in, and there was a rivalry between users to gain attention through the harshest comments. Politicians from across the board reached out to me. Some of them did not support what I'd said. Economic Freedom Fighters (EFF) leader Julius Malema said, 'My sister, I do not agree with what you said, but stop responding now.' His followers, intending to degrade me, liked to call me a 'tea-girl for Mandela'. But on this occasion, I appreciated him reaching out in a civilised manner and showing a little compassion, even though we disagreed on many things. My ignorant Twitter outburst showed me how divided people had become again, despite Madiba's efforts to unite us behind a common goal for the good of all South Africans.

When I woke up the next morning, Sunday, I felt wrung out and exhausted. Nonetheless, I decided, I had to do this talk. It would be extremely damaging for me to cancel at such a late stage. I simply had to face myself, even though I felt deeply ashamed and tearful.

I again managed to find my way to the theatre. I was supposed to talk about forgiveness, peace and reconciliation, and to recount the story of my first meeting with Madiba. My presentation had a strong anti-racism message, yet I now stood accused of racism. I didn't know if I was qualified to argue against that. I took a few deep breaths as I stood in the wings before it was my turn to go on stage, and I pressed my nails into my hands with as much force as possible to try to control my emotions. I started with a short disclaimer that English was not my first language. As I said this, a thought struck me: perhaps if I'd tweeted in Afrikaans, my mother tongue, I would have expressed myself better and in a kinder way.

I was on stage in front of more than 1 500 people. I had to mean what I was about to say. As the words left my mouth, they slowly also registered in my mind. Could I hold the meaning of what I was saying in my consciousness? I was deeply emotional and, as I retold the story of my first meeting with Madiba, I felt my eyes fill with tears and a burning sensation in my heart. I was devastated that what I'd done would have disappointed Madiba, and I yearned for him intensely. I had been insensitive and inconsiderate, and that was not the person he'd taught me to be. But as I spoke about his ability to forgive, I realised that the long road to forgive myself was ahead of me. When I quoted him talking about love being more powerful than hate, I found solace in his words.

At the conclusion of my talk, the crowd warmly applauded. Afterwards, my book was on sale (it sold out) and I spent the next few hours signing copies and conversing with people. For a blissful short while, I forgot about the storm back home.

When I left the theatre, I entered the first coffee shop I saw. I sat down and called my brother. I wanted to ask him to contact my parents; they were not tech-savvy, so I couldn't message them directly to reassure them. I didn't want them to be overly concerned, and I had to play down the situation. They had no idea what Twitter was but would have seen the media reports. No matter your age or relationship with your mother, in times of distress or illness, you just want to give up for a while and surrender to your mother's care. I longed for that, but the full weight of this catastrophe would be too much for her to bear.

I thought that when my brother answered, he would have some consolation for me. But he didn't. He was clearly in shock too: 'What de hell is going on?' It was his angry voice, which I'd never liked. 'Your name is on the front page of every newspaper,' he scolded. My safety net – my brother – was also angry at me. But, in fact, he was concerned for me more than anything else. It was masked by the anger, a defence mechanism we'd both learnt from an early age.

Next I called my brother-in-law and asked him to take over my Twitter account. He changed my passwords so I would stop engaging with trolls and trying to defend myself, but mainly so I'd be shielded from the brutality. I simply couldn't help myself, and I was particularly bad at choosing who to engage with. He knew that I wouldn't stop until I was stopped. I do love a good fight, but it's distasteful and unnecessary to sling insults and arguments at people who, through anonymity, do not even have the courage to stand by their own words.

Much later, he told me that he felt as if he needed a mental enema to wash away the crude language and insults he'd seen hurled at me: misogyny, sexism, racism – all of it.

My assistant back home started responding to requests for interviews, explaining that I was abroad on business and unable to engage. I realised that whatever I said would add fuel to the fire. My job now was to withdraw and reflect deeply on what I'd done.

As I walked back to the hotel, I felt like an old garment that was pulling apart at the seams. Once the adrenaline from being on stage had subsided, all I wanted was to pass out and never wake up again. I crawled into my hotel bed and sobbed, replaying the highs and the lows of the last six months in my mind.

December 2014.

Five months after my memoir came out, the publisher, Penguin, chose it as their book of the year. I was deeply grateful that people from all walks of life were interested in reading about my journey with Madiba.

Random people stopped me in the street, their eyes filled with tears, often taking my hand or wanting to hug me. I cried with many of them and laughed with others about the funny stories I'd shared. It was an emotional time for me, as so many of my memories of Madiba were triggered. Some people would give me a clap on the back or kiss me, and on more than one occasion I had to dig deep not to tell them that I didn't like being touched by strangers. Madiba had to endure this too, in an exaggerated form, for so many years. But he was a people's person. He got his energy from people. I was the complete opposite. The touching and hugging and kissing made me feel even more alone. Neither Madiba nor Professor Jakes Gerwel – his closest advisor – were there for me to share my private thoughts about gestures like these. We had often laughed about people's strange behaviour, so unguarded and beautifully innocent, yet sometimes so intrusive. I felt vulnerable and exposed. But my deep sense of personal loss at Madiba's passing – something I was not equipped to deal with – was overtaken by a gruelling travel schedule, which included book launches in France, the UK and the US.

All the media attention was overwhelming, but for a brief period I enjoyed my publicists taking over the running of my life. I loved the South African book launch, which was in June 2014, but deliberately skipped the country afterwards to avoid attention and went straight into the European launch tour.

On a train from Paris to London, I was admiring the beauty that came with the European summer: endless fields of purple lavender, followed by lush green lawns surrounded by mountains and streams kissing the edges of forests. I was mesmerised. My heart was smiling. I was proud of my book and happy that people shared that joy. There, on that train, I was enjoying the anonymity – and, for the first time in over twenty years of travel, I was simply enjoying myself. Until I checked my phone.

I had a message from an ex-colleague who was working for a prominent law firm in Johannesburg, telling me that a senior partner of the firm – someone I considered a close associate – had been alerted to the fact that the Nelson Mandela Foundation wanted an assessment of my book to see whether I'd breached confidentiality.

'I'm sorry, repeat that, please,' I said when the senior partner called. I was feeling upbeat after the launch in Paris of the French translation of my book, but that evaporated in an instant. The blood drained from my face. 'The foundation that helped me with the book, that proofread the book, are now questioning the confidentiality?' I clarified.

Madiba, Prof Gerwel and I had set up the foundation as a post-presidential office, but it soon became a vehicle for Madiba's schools and clinics projects and the 46664 Aids campaign (466/64 had been his Robben Island prison number) and then a centre for dialogue. It was also where memorabilia and his body of work were being held for safekeeping. After Madiba's passing, it focused on creating a safe space for difficult dialogue between parties, in addition to being a library project, organising Mandela Day and hosting exhibitions.

'Yes,' came the affirmation from the attorney. It was hurtful that my own former employer, having made several corrections to the manuscript, would now turn against me without warning. At the same time, I knew that there was no confidentiality breach whatsoever. As already mentioned, lawyers had checked the manuscript carefully before publication. Only one edit was made on the advice of a senior counsel.

Another legal firm confirmed that there was no basis for challenging my book. But the incident destroyed the joy I'd felt during the launch period, and a dark cloud of uncertainty descended on me. I later learnt from foundation staff that a lone voice from the board of trustees had expressed reservations about the book.

With all this going on, I lost sight of the complications my memoir brought to my personal life. I hardly had time for myself and, although I loved every minute of the promotion tour, it meant I had no time to process what had happened – other than the reminiscing I'd done during the writing process.

What I'd lost sight of was that, despite most South Africans feeling a sense of loss and sadness at Madiba's death, the hardened racists would not be softened by a book. Most people who are open to change also read: they seek knowledge and exposure to better themselves rather than being stuck with the same mindset their entire lives. The loudest criticism came from people who hadn't read my book. They simply did not read any books. Ever.

With the publication of a memoir, a chorus of complaints, accusations and falsehoods often follows. My experience was no different. Despite stating unequivocally – and in thirteen different languages – that I did not claim to be the only person to have worked for Nelson Mandela, and that a much bigger group deserved credit, the first accusation after the publication of the book was: 'So she pretends she was the only one who worked for him.' Although I haven't read *Good Morning, Mr Mandela* again recently, I'm quite sure that I made the opposite clear within the first ten pages. I credited the people that I'd worked with and those I had employed to assist and support me, and I thanked everyone in the extended workforce for their contributions to Madiba's life. Initially, I tried to rebut certain allegations, but I quickly realised it was impossible to force someone to read, let alone comprehend.

Social media also delivered renewed attacks from conservative white South Africans who called me names and attacked Madiba's legacy. Comments included 'stop idolising a terrorist', 'you worship a bomb planter', 'we see you hate white people', and 'you sold out, you k***boetie' (a derogatory racist word classified as hate speech and used during apartheid to demean people, followed by the Afrikaans word for 'brother'). These attacks preceded a list of things Madiba had allegedly done – while he was locked up in prison on Robben Island off the coast of Cape Town and allowed to write only one letter every six months. Ja-nee, I sighed, they'll come up with anything now that he's dead and can no longer defend himself. These attacks increased when the book became such a big success. The critics were in the minority, but they were loud and relentless.

In 2014, Twitter was taking off and I often found myself – me, a white Afrikaner – single-handedly trying to defend Madiba's legacy. I ended up arguing with anonymous accounts. First mistake! Never argue with anonymous accounts or people who are not prepared to take on a fight without a mask. In my experience, they'll simply try to bully you.

It was December and people were on holiday, taking a break from their phones and social media (the selfie had not yet become a thing). I'd spent most of 2014 touring and promoting my book, and only once the country had shut down for the holidays did I begin the mourning process – a year after Madiba's death. When *Rapport* picked it as the book of the year, the attacks gained oxygen. 'Don't pay attention to the critics,' many people told me. But it *was* personal, and it hurt.

I remember Zindzi Mandela, Madiba's younger daughter with his second wife, Winnie, defending me during several onslaughts from these anonymous radicals. It felt as if moderates – people with sense and an appreciation for Madiba's role in history – were driving past the proverbial accident scene on Twitter, slowing down to look but not interested enough to stop for fear of being implicated or having to get involved. While I was energised by the outpouring of love and good wishes, I felt worn out by the consistent attacks from pure racists.

I felt responsible for being unable to move them or soften their hearts, and I had probably hoped they would realise that even if you differed politically from Nelson Mandela, you could still recognise how he had made humanity shine.

'The biggest mistake this country made was to release Mandela,' I often heard – usually from people who yearned for apartheid and refused to realise that, had it not been for Madiba's leadership, many of them would not be alive. There would probably have been an all-out civil war, with huge loss of life on both sides. Had this happened, it's unlikely that the battlefield would have been restricted to borders or military camps; it would have penetrated communities and middle-class homes, too.

Our differences, and the conflict, seemed insurmountable at the time. But leadership and determination to come to a negotiated settlement prevailed. Over a period of 100 days, while we and the world were celebrating South Africa's new democracy, more than 800 000 people were killed in the Rwandan genocide – something that could easily have been our destiny.

After New Year, I desperately needed a break from being in the public eye. I also had to prepare for my TEDx talk in mid-January 2015, so I decided to travel with a friend to Mauritius, where we stayed with a wonderful couple. Unfortunately, as soon as we arrived, the island was shut down due to a cyclone. We were forced to shelter indoors the entire week of our much-anticipated holiday.

We mostly read and relaxed but were frustrated as our holiday plans to swim every day, soak up the sun and enjoy the wonderful tropical climate were hampered by the weather. Instead of feeling fresh and rested for my speaking engagement, I felt drained and roughed up. I'd really needed the sun and warm waters to wash away the negativity that had hijacked my mind amid the constant social media attacks and the backlash against my book. I was being mocked, and the more the government messed up and politicians misbehaved, the louder the chorus against my book. On top of that, the South African economy was under pressure and a full-blown economic crisis was looming. My anger festered while the storm raged outside. I'd hoped to regain my equilibrium but I found myself in the spin cycle of a washing machine on an island in the Indian Ocean.

And rather than disconnecting from what was going on back home, I kept up to date. All this achieved was to make me feel as frustrated as hell while accusations were being thrown about during the ANC's anniversary celebrations. The ANC usually marks its annual 8th of January birthday with a rally. In 2015, the 103rd anniversary, the celebrations took place on 10 January, and the president of the ANC and the country, Jacob Zuma, delivered the birthday message – a copy of which I read while on my so-called holiday.

We travelled back to Johannesburg on 13 January, and I left for England the following evening. I was going to address a British audience, largely because of the success of my book. But I was acutely aware that South Africans, including me, were increasingly frustrated by what had happened in the previous week, months and recent years. It was something that I could not and would not deny, despite the 'good news' my book was trying to spread.

As I made my way to the airport, I desperately wished that, despite the inclement weather in Mauritius, I could have switched myself off from the political soapie back home. Cooped up inside, I'd ruminated on what President Zuma had said at the ANC anniversary celebrations and on the general state of malaise in South Africa. In March 2014, the public protector at the time, Advocate Thuli Madonsela, released her final report on the R246-million worth of 'security' upgrades at Zuma's homestead in the rural area of Nkandla in KwaZulu-Natal. The damning report found that South African taxpayer money had been misappropriated and squandered to pay for exorbitant upgrades to his house, while his henchmen tried to convince the public that one of the 'upgrades', a swimming pool, was built without the president having any knowledge of it or even asking who would pay for it. When this explanation was too implausible for people to swallow, the public was then told that the pool was a security feature – a 'fire pool'! The story changed faster than a fly loses its concentration.

I'd met Madonsela on a few occasions and remembered the time she'd visited Qunu, Madiba's homestead in the rural Eastern Cape, as part of her investigation – in order to compare security upgrades at the two presidential homesteads and their related costs. The security improvements to Madiba's house had cost a fraction of the Nkandla bill.

The public was divided over what some media outlets dubbed Nkandlagate. It was not fashionable to criticise the president, and if you did, you were ostracised and politically isolated for doing so. We just had to suck it up. He had the ANC's backing, and whatever he did was vehemently defended by those he'd strategically chosen to surround him. After all, he (via state coffers, of course) was essentially paying his disciples' salaries.

Today we know, based on the findings of the State Capture Commission led by Judge Raymond Zondo, that large-scale state capture was in the making and that Madonsela's first report was merely the tip of the iceberg.

People on the streets were feeling the degeneration of service delivery and, while most were still optimistic about the future, it was becoming clear that there was no alleviation of large-scale poverty, hunger and homelessness for people who'd been waiting some twenty years for the government to deliver on the promises it made when it came into power in 1994. Something wasn't right.

Although the ANC government had inherited a bankrupt state – a large debt bill had accrued to maintain apartheid, a niggly little detail conservatives conveniently chose to forget when they recited the list of corruption cases involving current politicians – the economy was growing, and forecasts showed that it was possible to deliver on many of the promises made to the electorate. In the fifteen years between 1994 and 2009 the ANC government made huge advances to get us out of bankruptcy. It paid all apartheid-era debts and managed to turn a 7,1 per cent deficit in 1992/93 into a budget surplus of 0,9 per cent in 2007/08, halving our debt burden from 49,5 per cent of GDP in 1995/96 to 26 per cent in 2008/09. But as a result of irresponsible public spending and ostentatious squandering of money by public servants (with the president at the forefront), the economy was in trouble and we all felt it in our daily lives.

Despite the public protector's report, Zuma was elected for a second presidential term just a few months after its release. Madonsela had to endure the wrath of the ANC and Zuma's supporters. She was verbally abused and belittled, challenged and mocked. But she has a thick skin and managed to heal herself through her work after the ordeal, becoming one of the strongest influencers of modern society in South Africa – a thought leader and a change maker.

On the odd occasion, Zuma was booed at public events, such as during a football match between South Africa's Bafana Bafana and Brazil in March 2014. Yet his close circle of advisors and most ANC members remained mum, reassuring him that he was the king of their hearts. The resistance to his position in the Presidency would later grow to the point where he was ousted. But more about that later.

During an ANC fundraising dinner on Friday, 9 January, held to coincide with the party's 2015 anniversary celebrations, Zuma was his jovial self, playing to the crowd who'd paid thousands of rand to attend and were probably anticipating a message of hope and renewal. The attendees were mostly influential businesspeople who could move the financial markets.

As had happened so often before, Zuma began with a lesson in colonialism, stating: 'You must remember that a man called Jan van Riebeeck arrived here on 6 April 1652, and that was the start of the trouble in this country.' He was referring to the arrival of the

Dutch East India Company commander tasked with establishing a refreshment station at the Cape. Yes, it eventually led to colonisation, but Zuma's statement was a one-dimensional view of South Africa's history, probably designed to deflect attention from the ANC's failures.

He made no mention of the multitude of problems facing the country, among them the escalating electricity crisis that resulted in large-scale blackouts – known as loadshedding – that were negatively affecting the already limping economy. There was no simple cause and effect, but the pitiful state of our electricity parastatal, Eskom, could at least in part be attributed to corruption. In his anniversary speech the next day, as reported in a 12 January 2015 *Daily Maverick* article titled 'Wash, Rinse, Repeat: Jacob Zuma's play-it-again birthday speech', the president shifted the blame (again): 'The belief out there is this [the energy crisis] is a result of failure of government or a lack of leadership in the country. The reality is the legacy of apartheid.'

While he was correct in saying that the power facilities were created during apartheid to 'serve a few', it was more complex than that, and his statement was only a fragment of the truth. What Zuma ought to have acknowledged is that the existing infrastructure had not been maintained, and that even the two new power stations under construction would not provide enough power to keep the economy going. As he dished out half-truths to the public, I was reminded of the many occasions that he'd done the same while visiting Madiba.

At some point while Zuma was in exile, he had been deputy chief representative of the ANC in Mozambique. Ronnie Kasrils, a minister in Madiba's cabinet and a founding member of the ANC's armed wing, Umkhonto we Sizwe (MK), spent time with Zuma in Mozambique. In his book *A Simple Man: Kasrils and the Zuma Enigma*, he recounts an event that took place on the border between Mozambique and Swaziland (now Eswatini) in 1982. When trying to cross no-man's land, they had to climb over the first border fence but Kasrils fell and sprained his ankle. With Zuma's help, he got over the second fence and crossed into Swaziland, where they expected some comrades to pick them up. It started raining and Kasrils produced two plastic sheets from his knapsack to shield them. He describes how they lay 'breathing in tandem' and generating heat from the close proximity of their bodies. Their lift didn't arrive, and they had to return to Mozambique, with 'Baba' (an affectionate way of referring to an elder in black culture) supporting him all the way. In Mozambique, they went to the house of one of 'Zuma's women' as Kasrils describes in his book. Once they were comfortable, he heard Zuma in the kitchen complaining to the woman about the 'stupid white man' he claimed had been responsible for their setback that night – even though they'd arrived at the pickup point long before the agreed time for the rendezvous. In his book, Kasrils also refers to many instances of distrust and paranoia that had set in at agencies within the ANC and government by the time Zuma came to power.

Jacob Zuma became the deputy president of South Africa in 1999, in the office of President Thabo Mbeki, Madiba's successor. He retained his position following general elections in 2004, but Mbeki dismissed him in June 2005 after his friend and business partner Schabir Shaik was convicted of fraud. In December of the same year, Zuma was charged with rape by a family friend and, after a widely publicised trial, was acquitted. It was also during this time that several people at South Africa's intelligence agencies took part in the fabrication of emails implicating Zuma's political opponents in a smear campaign against Zuma, using tribalism to spread hate and division. They fostered the belief that there was a conspiracy against Zuma, which was in fact self-orchestrated to build a support base. The ploy paid off, and in 2007, Zuma was elected ANC president, which paved the way for him to become president of the country in 2009.

People like to point out that Madiba supported Zuma in his bid for the position of deputy president and later for the presidency. 'How could he have supported Zuma?' I'm asked outright. My response is usually that the Zuma presented to us at one-on-one meetings with Madiba was not the same Zuma we know now. His ambitions and greed were carefully obscured by his apparent openness and his ability to present to his audience whatever was best suited to the moment.

In his address at the ANC's 2015 anniversary, Zuma cherry-picked the populist parts of the Freedom Charter, adopted at the Congress of the People in Kliptown, a suburb of Soweto, in 1955. The document was the backbone of the revolution against white domination in South Africa. He quoted the preamble: 'We, the people of South Africa, declare for all our country and the world to know: that South Africa belongs to all who live in it, black and white, and that no government can justly claim authority unless it is based on the will of all the people . . .' (I remember first reading these words, and falling in love with them, in 1994 after I started working for President Mandela. Now, as Zuma quoted them, I couldn't help feeling that familiar patriotism that Madiba had awoken in me.)

His speech continued: 'We are committed to building a South African nation that is diverse . . . It is our task to work together to foster social cohesion and build a common South African nationhood . . .

'Let us therefore give meaning to "service to the people" and serve them with humility and dignity.' (If only this were true, I thought. There was no service to the people, only to a select few, and there was no humility or dignity).

'We must take charge of how we shape the future of the ANC. Let us rededicate ourselves to the core values of the ANC. These are unity, selflessness, sacrifice, collective leadership, humility, honesty, discipline, hard work, internal debates, constructive criticism and self-criticism and mutual respect . . .

'We are calling on all our members to actively promote all rights and freedoms and to fight all forms of discrimination, in all its manifestations.' (Absolutely bloody full marks to the speech writer. It pulls at every heartstring and takes you through the full range of emotions, just like your favourite song does with a soothing melody and beautiful lyrics.)

The rest of his speech touched on corruption – the ANC should take the lead in ending it; the ANC government's achievements in improving living conditions and making 'unprecedented progress' in delivering basic services 'to millions who were denied these services by apartheid and colonial regimes'; and a hot potato, crime – there was a decline in serious crime but it remained a 'major societal and economic challenge'.

No surprises there, given that even Jackie Selebi, the former national commissioner of the South African Police Service and president of Interpol from 2004 to 2008, was convicted of corruption in 2010, after a four-year investigation, and sentenced to fifteen years in prison. Gerrie Nel, chief prosecutor for the Scorpions special investigative unit, who had brought charges against Selebi, was himself arrested and charged in 2008. He was then released and the charges were dropped. In 2009, when the Selebi trial began, Nel was the one leading the charges. What preceded the outcome, though, was a confusing stream of what appeared to be political meddling and misinformation.

On any given day in South Africa, you'll be surprised by the new depths of intrigue. I share this background because it's important to understand the political manoeuvring at the time. Nothing was what it seemed, and many people were being taken in by propaganda, like during the apartheid years. Censorship was the norm when I was growing up, which meant I discovered the truth about what was happening in South Africa only many years later.

Ordinary folks were feeling discouraged, and I – unjustifiably – felt as if I carried the burden of pointing out how Zuma was lying to us. Naturally, this put me in the firing line.

But I was not the only one: Max du Preez was also a target. He'd founded the *Vrye Weekblad* newspaper in 1988, at the height of apartheid, to counter the misinformation and propaganda that was being fed to the public by media outlets that were not just censored, but in many instances also acted as a mouthpiece of the state. I'd met him occasionally in passing, but I greatly respected him when I learnt that he was one of very few brave Afrikaners who refused to be silenced by the apartheid regime.

In December 2014, a month before the ANC's annual celebrations, Max had written an opinion piece, which first appeared in the *Pretoria News*, in which he criticised Zuma for the havoc he was causing in South Africa. He called him a 'one-man wrecking ball' and claimed that the devastation he'd caused would take years to repair.

Max wrote that in addition to inflicting serious damage on our political culture and key institutions, Zuma had 'masterfully out-manoeuvred those who stood up to him and instilled a culture of fear in this party [the ANC]'. He continued:

> He richly rewarded those loyal to him through a vast system of patronage and massively enriched his own family and clan ... The golden thread running through his six years as president was his determination to stay out of court (and jail) with more than 700 charges of corruption, fraud and racketeering hanging over his head.
>
> In the process he co-opted and corrupted the entire intelligence machinery, the National Prosecuting Authority, the police service and the SABC [South African Broadcasting Corporation]. Tender-preneurship blossomed and corruption mushroomed with almost no consequences for perpetrators ...

'It is Zuma Demolition Inc at work,' Max concluded.

What followed was an avalanche of catastrophic proportions.

The Presidency responded with a statement refuting all the allegations, ending with: 'What is more disturbing is that the piece smacks of prejudice and racism given the manner in which Mr du Preez describes the President.' It also said the Presidency was alarmed by the personal attack on Zuma. This didn't sound like a response in a constitutional democracy where people enjoy freedom of expression, but rather one in a dictatorship in which you dare not criticise the president.

Throughout the December holiday and into the new year, with a renewed focus on Zuma during the celebrations, Max was trending on Twitter and blatantly being called a racist. He quit his column with Independent Media after then group executive editor Karima Brown issued an apology to the president on behalf of the newspaper without Max's knowledge or consent.

Over the same period, former president FW de Klerk was being honoured in the opposition-run metro of the City of Cape Town with a proposal to name a five-kilometre stretch of road after him. He had jointly received the Nobel Peace Prize in 1993 with Nelson Mandela following the peaceful negotiations in South Africa that led to the first democratic elections in 1994. Despite this, there was an uproar in response to Cape Town's proposal.

I spent the day after returning from my Mauritian 'holiday' changing suitcases and running errands before heading back to the airport to fly to the UK. I realise now that my busy schedule, the political decline in South Africa and the constant public onslaught on me meant I had not yet really reflected on Madiba's passing. I hadn't given myself time to grieve and have the loss sink in, and the holiday had not helped.

Yet, when I took my seat on the Emirates aeroplane, I felt at ease, with a pleasant undertone of excitement. I watched a movie, had dinner and went to sleep. I woke up to go to the bathroom during the night, and when I got back to my seat, I started reading the international news headlines on the mini TV screen in front of me. A headline about South Africa kept popping up every few seconds: 'Jacob Zuma blames apartheid for South Africa's problems'. An unfortunate headline, enough to get my blood boiling. To make things worse, the headline was, like my thoughts and everything else 35 000 feet above ground, on repeat. I couldn't go back to sleep. Instead, I worked myself up into an unhealthy state of anger as I thought back to events of the past weeks, months and years in South Africa.

Had I seen the headline on some other day or on some other flight, perhaps it wouldn't have upset me as it did. My reaction was sponta-neous and unfiltered; I was convinced of my own righteousness. Against the backdrop of being attacked about my place in Madiba's life, history being blamed for all our current-day failures, Max being called a racist, De Klerk being repeatedly vilified, loadshedding and the associated job losses, a floundering economy, an increase in un-employment and the daily suffering of a large proportion of South Africans, plus a holiday gone horribly wrong, the headline was the impetus for my anger to erupt.

I'd caught wind of what the media was picking up on when I scanned the news before leaving home. I'd also read Zuma's formal, typed-up speech for the ANC celebrations while I was in Mauritius. Very little of it was rooted in reality. Yet, most ANC supporters still believed that Zuma and the ANC government were doing great. Or so they said.

Madiba taught me that blame is a useless concept as it doesn't change the reality of the past. But we must acknowledge the past to remind ourselves where we come from and to ensure that history never repeats itself. It should not, however, be used as a scapegoat to mask mismanagement, incompetence or corruption.

These attacks on people had one thing in common: they were all about race. In a country like ours, it will always be about race. The difference is that during the Madiba era we were able to talk about the past without slaughtering one another. We could also focus on the future, because that's what our leader did. And people imitate their leaders.

Then, in 2015, Zuma was dragging us back to 1652. For my part, I acknowledge that I hadn't really thought about the skewed view of history we'd been taught at school, in which Jan van Riebeeck was assigned heroic status as a kind of founding father of South Africa. What the history books omitted was that the arrival of the Dutch at the Cape had set in motion a catalogue of injustice, including slavery, land appropriation and the exploitation of indigenous people. Yes, there *were* already people living at the Cape, along the coast and further inland – people who had called this land home for centuries.

While my understanding of the world had changed dramatically since I'd started working for Madiba, it didn't erase the falsehoods that had been entrenched in my culture for generations. I'm only half of Dutch descent; my paternal forefathers were some of the first French Huguenots to arrive at the Cape in 1688, so we missed the Van Riebeeck ship. Yet, here I am. Had it not been for them, I would not be able to call this country mine by birth. The Protestant Huguenots fled persecution by the Catholics in Europe, and some smart alec probably told the captain of our ship that South Africa was the place to go.

It's often believed that all white Afrikaans people in South Africa come from a long line of farmers – 'boere' in Afrikaans. But there were no farmers among my forebears. The Frenchman Pierre Grange, to whom I trace my ancestry, was a mason. I can't even keep a bunch of parsley alive, and there's clearly no trace of the knowledge or skill of farming in my family.

I don't feel protective of Van Riebeeck, and I certainly never had a conversation about him with Madiba. But it riled me that his arrival on our shores was being blamed for all manner of problems more than 350 years later.

And so, sitting on the plane, my irritation grew as the night passed.

I mulled over the frustration of ordinary people in South Africa who found it hard to cope with the regular electricity supply interruptions.

How do you bath and feed kids who need to go to school the next day without electricity at night? How do you study when you don't have light at night? Do you just give up, or do you study by candlelight? I also thought about the majority of people in South Africa who had lived without a power supply their entire lives – yes, as a result of apartheid. But this was twenty-one years later. Twenty-one years.

In hindsight, even 30 years is not enough to address the legacies of apartheid and colonialism, but we should guard against politicians and populists using it as an excuse to hide inefficiency and corruption.

As problems mounted for ordinary people, blame became the only currency among politicians who shied away from taking responsibility. There was no way that, out of pure loyalty, I could still defend the glorious movement to which Nelson Mandela had dedicated his life. Even though I'd never been a member of the ANC, I had felt allegiance to the party when Madiba was in office. Then, the possibilities and promises for a new South Africa were tangible.

My thoughts wandered to Max's opinion piece and how he was branded a racist for daring to speak out against the president. Then I thought about De Klerk and how people refused to accept that two contradictory things could be true in any story and about any person. I thought of how Madiba had given him credit for his willingness to work together to end apartheid but also spoken of the hard talk and losing his cool with De Klerk on many occasions during the negotiations.

We were a lazy bunch, I thought, refusing to think about things in life. When you highlight one positive aspect of someone's character, it doesn't mean that you're whitewashing history. No one is the result of a single mistake or a single achievement in life. We are complex, messy and full of contradictions.

As the night passed, I missed Madiba tremendously. He'd made me feel at home in South Africa. 'White people born in South Africa,' he'd said, 'have no other home but this country. This is their country too. You can discover where you come from but at the same time feel proud about your existence on this continent, for when you contribute to changing the reality as a result of the past, this place is yours too.' The words played over and over in my head. I could literally hear him.

The plane touched down at Heathrow, and I made my way to a long immigration queue. I was tired and irritated. When I switched on my phone data to check if anyone had messaged me overnight, the news of the debate in South Africa featured instantly. I went onto Twitter and saw that De Klerk, Du Preez and Van Riebeeck were still the talking points.

When would this stop, I wondered? When would the blaming stop? Politicians acted with impunity while blaming the past because the past could not enter the fray and argue or defend itself.

I didn't give it any more thought, and a string of tweets tumbled out. And then, to top it all: 'When is Jacob Zuma going to stop blaming the past for what is going on in South Africa? Just call me Jan van Riebeeck . . . OK.'

There's an unwritten rule never to tweet when you're angry. Big transgression.

I switched off my data and moved through immigration. As I was waiting for my luggage to arrive, I thought of another point I wanted to make and switched the data on again. I changed my profile name to Zelda van Riebeeck – without giving it a second thought. And, as we know, there's no 'sarcasm' button on Twitter.

After collecting my luggage, I found my driver and began the journey to Oxford. Only once during the trip did I briefly switch my data on again. I saw that my tweets had attracted attention, but I didn't want to read the comments yet. I was not aware that people were just waking up back home, and because it was a rainy day across the country, many were still in bed and on social media – all the ingredients for a perfect Twitter storm.

'We are going to deal with you,' some tweets read, and worse. I extended my trip purely out of fear and came back later than planned. The day I arrived, a friend had his security staff pick me up from the airport. Throughout the journey I had a burning need to apologise to him. I felt sick and wanted to slip quietly into my house without anyone knowing I was home. You don't know whether threats on Twitter are hollow or serious when you're thousands of miles away from home. But now that I was back in South Africa, I felt exposed.

Deeply ashamed, I remained undercover for a few days. I'd lost a considerable amount of work – people were cancelling my engagements and giving lame excuses for doing so rather than addressing the elephant in the room. It was only one of the large insurance companies that had the courage to tell me that the risk of having me speak at their national event was too big. They'd apparently had a discussion at board level about it. One of Madiba's closest allies who was on their board felt that insulting the sitting president was too much to bear.

I realised how much I missed Madiba. If I could just talk to him once more, I thought. If I could just feel the warmth of his smile consoling me. I knew that what I'd done would have angered him, but I also knew that he would have taken my hand and comforted me with his presence. I hadn't yet digested the fact that the person I'd lost had been so much more than just my employer. He had been like a grandfather to me and the very best mentor I could ever have wished for. Perhaps now was the time for me to explore the lessons embedded in my experiences with him.

Over the next few weeks, I continued to be harshly self-critical. Then, one day, I thought: I can't wake up on another morning hating myself like this. It's not getting better, and every day people still comment or write opinion pieces about my tweets. Anyone with any link to Nelson Mandela who appeared in public was asked for comment. And all those who hadn't been able to see Madiba often enough during his lifetime, or who'd wanted his endorsement or attendance at an event but whose requests were declined, saw this as an opportunity to settle their scores with me. My friends found it hard to keep me motivated. Some initially checked up on me every day, then every few days. But, while they had moved on from the Twitter debacle, I was not able to. I had to shut out the noise or I'd go mad, I thought. It followed me like my shadow, every second of the day. People recognised me at the supermarket, and I could see in their faces exactly what they thought of me.

I couldn't bear it. I contemplated bringing an end to my life. I just couldn't forgive myself for hurting innocent people with my words – not the Jacob Zumas of the world, but the people who hardly get by every month as they try to provide for their families. Their suffering was made worse by my unkind and thoughtless words. It was an insult to them to use my race to demonstrate that whites were being bullied when, in fact, black people were being bullied by the same government too. Who and what you were didn't matter to those in power. For a moment, I had been blinded by my anger and underestimated my individual power. I'd thought that no one paid attention to me anyway. Why was it so important what I said or what opinions I had on anything when I'd constantly been told, over a period of twenty years, how unimportant I was?

Now I was questioning my existence because of it.

Approaching a traffic light on my way home from the dry-cleaner one day, I thought: I'll just drive through this red light and see what happens. If I come out alive, I'll know that I'm supposed to stay.

I made it through the traffic light. It's not a challenge anyone should put to the universe.

I cried for days. The only other time that I had experienced such deep despair was when my engagement ended abruptly in 1993. Fortunately, five good friends carried me through and rescued me from myself. You cannot imagine ever getting up from an experience like that.

But, while I was trying to claw my way back from my ignorant Twitter outburst, there were also some who, instead of beating me down with words, extended a kind hand. Prof Hlengiwe Mkhize, an ANC deputy minister at the time, invited me for tea, and so did Songezo Zibi, former editor of *Business Day* newspaper and, at the time, a consultant at a major bank. (He went on to launch Rise Mzansi, the political party that contested the 2024 national elections.) These were complete strangers who gave me a safe space just to talk, with no explanations or apologies expected. Thuli Madonsela, then still public protector, made time to have lunch with me, and several prominent academics and political figures contacted me too.

Late one night, my phone rang. The caller ID showed it was 'Prof Jansen' – Jonathan Jansen, the renowned academic and government critic. My heart stopped as I was reminded of the late-night calls from Prof Jakes Gerwel (whom I called 'Prof') during Madiba's life, when we would catch up on what was happening in the office, freely criticise the government and politicians, and sometimes engage in, well, just good old gossiping. 'Nou't die politici dinge darem lelik opgefok, jong [Now the politicians have really fucked things up],' he would sometimes say, and I would burst out laughing. I was allowed to swear, but in my mind, a professor wasn't. He'd always been candid, and the same criticism he expressed privately he also dished out eagerly when he met with certain politicians in person. There were no holy cows.

Following the Twitter meltdown, the first call from Prof Jansen had come while I was on a layover in Dubai as I was returning from Oxford. He was comforting and calm as he consoled me. His follow-up calls were the same. I appreciated these gestures immensely. None of those who'd contacted me really knew me, but our interactions meant the world to me.

A few weeks later, I had to reapply for a UK visa for business engagements later in the year and scheduled an appointment at the visa agency in Pretoria. I didn't put on any makeup, tied my hair up in a bun and wore sunglasses to try to hide from my shame. I was still traumatised and trying to avoid people. Yes, a few had made contact, which I greatly appreciated, but the silence of those who couldn't be seen to publicly defend or support me, or at least my apology, was what hurt the most.

At the visa agency, I could see the disapproval of the white man, dressed in his khakis, who stood in front of me in the queue. He was clearly one of those angry at me for apologising and was probably calling me a 'slapgat' (a crude way of saying I was spineless) for what he had misinterpreted as an apology to Zuma. I could see the word in his eyes. Behind me in the queue was a young black woman. Our eyes connected, and I quickly looked away to avoid her glance and the embarrassment that it would bring if she recognised me. She had to be angry at me too, I thought. I was sandwiched between the two, and there was nowhere to run. I had to see this through, I told myself while desperately wanting to return to my car, or I'll never regain my confidence.

After my biometric information had been collected, the young woman stopped me on my way out. 'Are you Zelda?' she asked. 'Yes,' I replied, wincing and immediately stammering an apology. She didn't respond to my apology but said, 'Can I hug you, please?' Her eyes teared up, and mine followed suit. With tears rolling down my cheeks, I asked if she would mind if I waited for her so I could buy her a cup of coffee after her appointment. She agreed. She explained that she'd witnessed the whole ordeal on Twitter but was not able to defend me, as was the case with many others, because she worked for an international car company represented in South Africa and couldn't involve the company in the debate. She didn't consider my tweets racist – perhaps a little insensitive, but definitely not racist. I valued the time she'd taken to engage with me. Here I'd found a stranger, a black person, who dispelled my take on what I'd assumed was the response from *all* black people. She was a formidable career woman and a person of obvious great character. Our interaction put my ordeal in perspective, and she was one of the many people who restored my faith in myself and humanity.

I was reminded of a valuable lesson from Madiba: an ordinary person can change your life but also alter your thinking and experience. I'd been surrounded by some of the wisest and most influential people in the world, but the impact of an unlikely visitor along your life path can equally teach you an important lesson. Twitter is not the real world, I was repeatedly told. But it was only when people like her spoke to me that I realised that social media was, indeed, simply the worst reflection of any society.

One of the things that helped me find my feet and reclaim some self-worth was a special weekend event in Santa Fe, New Mexico, hosted by Amazon founder Jeff Bezos. I was surprised and excited when I received the invitation to the annual getaway, where Bezos gathers interesting people to interact, to share my experience of working with Madiba. It was 2016, and I'd had a year to heal from my bruising Twitter experience and cautiously emerge from my self-imposed cocoon. The group comprised about 80 people from all walks of life, both famous and ordinary. There was no distinction made between the super-rich and super-famous, those who'd simply had interesting experiences and those whose daily existence could serve to open people's eyes to a different reality.

Apart from socialising and spending time with legends like Billie Jean King, with whom you could play tennis if you wished, the weekend was filled with other activities. I opted to take part in horse-whispering because I love animals, and I thought it was something I couldn't fail at. It turned out to be way more than that: the horse taught me about boundaries. When our group entered the pasture where the horses were grazing, we were instructed to wait until a horse chose us – not the other way round. Each participant was then introduced to the group and asked what interpersonal challenge they were facing.

Despite my aversion to the invasion of my personal space – such as when strangers hug me or kiss me – I have a problem with setting and maintaining boundaries. I'm too open in allowing people into my private space. Then, when they come too close, I suffer from acute claustrophobia.

The handler showed me how to teach the horse to stay a specific distance from me. The horse stayed exactly where I'd left it. Then, after a few moments, I felt so sorry for the horse that I stepped closer or, through hand gestures, allowed it back into my space. It wasn't difficult to conclude that I was the problem, no one else. I had to learn that when I set boundaries, I needed to respect them myself, first and foremost, before expecting anyone else to do so.

I've improved a little, I think. It was just one of the insights I gained over the weekend – all of them appropriate to integrate into my life and pass on to others.

I'd been asked to address the gathering on the opening night. I admired the spectacular sunset as we sat around open fires on top of a hill. The atmosphere was electric with excitement, and I was nervous. We sipped slowly on authentic tequila, and everyone was friendly. People conversed and made small talk and, as I turned to greet another stranger, Michael Keaton removed a bug from my shoulder and joked about it. He was wearing a baseball cap and sunglasses, and I didn't recognise him. My companion was stunned that I didn't make a scene because the famous actor had just removed a bug from my shoulder. After meeting countless famous people over the years with Madiba, I was so desensitised to people's status in life that I honestly didn't know how to even pretend to be normal again. As I explained in *Good Morning, Mr Mandela*, I'd never really been affected by people's celebrity status. I also hadn't watch much television or many movies for most of the time I'd worked with Madiba. My knowledge of celebrity actors was limited to those who appeared in the classics, such as *The Godfather* and *The Shawshank Redemption*, as well as *Dirty Dancing* and some other popular films from the 1980s.

I didn't know who George RR Martin was – the screenwriter and novelist upon whose books the series *Game of Thrones* is based – and didn't immediately recognise actor Joseph Gordon-Levitt's name either. Perhaps my ignorance was a good thing: if I were intimidated by people's star status, I wouldn't be great at sharing my experiences. I had to delve deep and do justice to my story, I thought, without being affected by the fact that some of the most influential and famous people on earth were gathered in front of me. To top it all, many of them, including Shonda Rhimes (creator of the popular *Grey's Anatomy* TV series, among others) and actors Reese Witherspoon, Michael J Fox and Julianne Moore, specialised in brilliantly depicting other people's stories.

The evening breeze enveloped me as I sat on a bar stool at the fire, wrapped in a rich cloth of vibrant colours, as if Madiba was hugging me. I began to speak. Even in his absence, people were in awe of his humanity, humility, strength, courage and ability to forgive, and there was not a dry eye in the audience after my session. After sharing my story, I felt a strong sense of Madiba's profound influence on my life.

Much later, when reflecting on the insight I'd had when working with the horse, I realised that I'd forgotten how unequivocally clear Madiba's boundaries always were. He would tolerate a lot, but once he'd drawn the line, that was it. For example, when he had a falling-out with his attorney Ismail Ayob, the relationship was over. It was not a boundary Madiba ever allowed to be crossed.

He freely engaged his adversaries, and one could easily mistake his friendliness and the courtesy he showed – even when being attacked by others – as blind acceptance of their onslaught. When he was harshly criticised by ANC officials for pursuing people's right to access to HIV/Aids drugs, he accepted the criticism. I walked into his house one afternoon following his return from an ANC National Executive Committee meeting where senior leaders had attacked him. As he recalled what had been said, I could see that he was troubled by some of the insults that had been aimed at him. Yet, some time later, in an interview with Oprah Winfrey, he said that you had to commend people for their bravery in attacking you as a leader. He would be friendly in greeting and communicating with those who'd criticised him, but there would never be a close relationship between them again. The boundary had been set. I could see that there was a lesson for me about maintaining neutrality and walking away from situations and people without being tempted to enter the fray again or have the last word.

One of the best parts about that Santa Fe weekend was that there were strict instructions against using mobile phones. No one was allowed to take photos or post on social media. It made me realise that powerful people used social media as a tool, nothing more and nothing less. Respecting one another's privacy was a priceless shared commodity.

This sharpened my realisation that my behaviour on social media had not contributed to anything good in society. I'd been quick to comment on things that were none of my business. But I came to understand that just because you had the power to do something, it didn't mean you had to use that power. When waters are rough and murky, you struggle to see your own reflection. And when you're angry and emotional, it's the same. I was as much part of the problem as others were.

I also subsequently became aware that I sometimes spent hours scrolling through other people's lives, while I didn't scroll through my own. That time could be used more productively by investing in relationships, talking to the people in front of me and dealing with my own issues. (I'm still not going to have long telephone conversations, and I can't bring myself to engage in rambling chit-chats. Just saying.)

Elaine Moore, columnist for the *Financial Times*, commented: 'Social media networks are not very sociable these days. Instead of talking to one another, we have become mostly silent onlookers.' With that comes measuring ourselves and our problems against a make-believe reality. No one posts just about their problems, so we know very little about the real-life struggles of people we admire. When I put these people and their lives on a pedestal, my gratitude for my own life diminished. Now I continuously remind myself not to get hooked on the fantasy – and, importantly, to stay out of other people's business whenever I feel an urge to comment on something that really doesn't concern me.

The verbal battering I'd endured during my ignorant Twitter out-burst was brutal. Now, looking back with the advantage of time and distance, I find it interesting to observe someone else's entirely diffe-rent experience. In a string of tweets, Giulietta Talevi, the money and investing editor at the *Financial Mail* at the time, commented:

> When you wake to a massive water leak from outside your house, flowing into it, with loadshedding on the go, having gone to bed with loadshedding, is when you want to give up, and get the hell out of here.
>
> What happened to the ANC's commitment to non-racialism? Or, um, diversity in the party ranks? Silly me! All whites are obviously like that pair of Free State yahoos. [Referring to a group of white men who had assaulted a black child at a holiday resort over Christmas]. Nothing to contribute, nothing to offer (other than taxes obvs).

When questioned by a fellow journalist about her reference to tax, she said, 'I'm not making the point that only whites pay taxes. I think that's entirely obvious. I'm making a sarcastic point that it seems the only valuable aspect of whites, to the ANC, is their tax contribution to the fiscus.'

The responses to her tweets were minimal. People had moved on, and the 'violent version of the Mexican wave' called cancel culture was busy taking someone else down at the time.

The difference was that my tweets had been sent in 2015 and hers in 2022. A lot had happened in between.

Although the bitterly painful lessons I learnt from my Twitter experience have helped me modify my social media behaviour, they didn't make me free of fault. I've made many mistakes subsequently, and I'm sure I'll continue to make many more. In April 2024, I did another TEDx talk, this time in Porto, a coastal town in Portugal. During the fifteen-minute presentation, I made a few mistakes due to technical issues. Afterwards, I realised they were all I remembered from the talk. Such is life. You struggle to focus on anything other than the mistakes – not only yours but also those of others. I try to remind myself that Madiba was particularly good at insisting on full recognition of the complexity of all human beings – warts and all, as they say.

But when I was under attack amid the Twitter drama, that was furthest from my mind. Especially when some people chose to throw an extra punch by asking: have you learnt nothing from Nelson Mandela?

At the time, this cut to the quick. But once I'd managed to soften the sharp edge of my shame and self-criticism, I began to contemplate the question – in kinder terms.

Most people will agree that Madiba left an incredible legacy. Your legacy is not about the material possessions you leave behind but how you're remembered, and you don't have to be famous to leave a legacy. A social media footprint or a good PR strategy is not what creates a legend. It creates influencers, but influencers come and go. Madiba touched lives; he is cherished and remembered.

I called him Khulu – 'grandfather' in his mother tongue, isiXhosa; he called me Zeldina and considered me an honorary granddaughter. He showed me that our interesting differences were far less important than our common humanity. A legend leaves an indelible impression on others, and I wanted to find out whether I, as someone who had been so close to him, truly comprehended what that impression comprised. What did I actually learn? And had I sufficiently embodied those lessons from Madiba so that I could reflect on them?

Exploring those questions led to this book.

PART I

Who am I without Madiba?

For nineteen years, Madiba filled my days. Every day was dedicated to him. Holidays or birthdays, they were all his. My life was structured around his needs, his movements and his agenda. I was always available. Today, many people talk about the importance of work–life balance, but there was nothing like that during my time at Madiba's side. I willingly dedicated my every waking hour to him, and sometimes my sleeping hours too. He would call any time of the day or night to ask to be reminded of something, or to remind me of something he wanted done.

He knew very well that nothing was ever too much trouble for me, and attending to his needs was my calling. He knew that, because of the amount of time we'd spent together, I could always anticipate what he would require next. When you work with someone so closely, you tend to adopt a lot of their behaviour, which makes it easy for you to read any situation. But in all things, his presence was clear and focused.

At the time I didn't consciously assess his characteristics; I was simply overburdened with tasks, pressure and to-do lists. Being the so-called gatekeeper to the most famous and revered statesman of our time, I was constantly in survival mode and didn't have time to think about my own interpretation of things.

But in a very unassuming way, Madiba became my moral compass through his presence in my life. I was acutely aware of how things were done around him, the optics and how it mattered. I was consciously seeking the right way to do everything, and whenever I was in doubt, I knew I could freely ask. His guiding principles of empathy, compassion and respect were the values my parents had imprinted on me, too, but their versions were skewed by the political isolation caused by apartheid.

Madiba had played a central role in my life since 1994. After his death, I felt his absence acutely. It was easy, while he was alive, to live like him, be like him and act like him because he inspired me by setting a clear and sound example every single day. It flowed naturally, from being so close to him, to emulate the values and principles that he stood for.

Now that he'd gone, my true north had faded and, being under pressure, I had failed to allow his influence to dictate my behaviour. I had slipped back into my own selfish and inconsiderate ways, thinking about what was best for me as opposed to what was best for us. His calling was a selfless devotion to humanity, and in his absence mine had turned back to how I perceived myself, how I defended myself and how I viewed my problems rather than ours – that is, all South Africans.

After Madiba's death, I felt an intense sense of loss. I'd also lost my own grandparents by then and a few good friends who'd died too soon, but this loss was different. I felt confused about my role in life. What was I supposed to be and do now that I was no longer part of his life?

The phones stopped ringing and my usefulness to people diminished once the association with Madiba was gone. It's not something I regret. I quickly discovered who had been truly invested in my life and who had been there for the occasion. I've no doubt obliviously done the same to people in my orbit. There's no blame. It is what it is.

When you're loved by someone and you have such a special relationship, the loss is intense. Madiba believed that I was strong and fearless – even if I did not believe so myself – and his confidence in me made me achieve things I'd never imagined I was capable of. And my blessing was to have been loved by him.

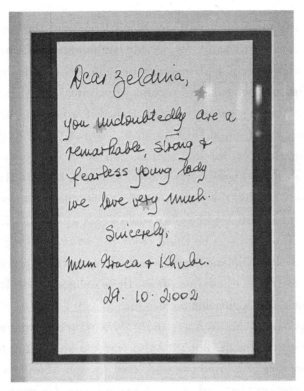

Dear Zeldina,

you undoubtedly are a
remarkable, strong &
fearless young lady
we love very much.

Sincerely,

Mum Graca & Khulu.

29. 10. 2002

My most prized possession – being loved and appreciated by Madiba and Mrs Machel.

The memories of Madiba ebb and flow like the ocean. Not a day goes by without me thinking of him. I feel disappointed in the government and the ANC for allowing his legacy to be squandered and questioned through fraud, corruption and mismanagement. My country's slide into the abyss, away from principle, purpose and ubuntu, is personal and painful. I and many others were part of an era when South Africa blossomed.

For so many years, Madiba – and Graça Machel for some years after they married on his 80th birthday – was my family too. I miss our holidays together, even though I was half working the whole time. Mauritius was a favourite destination; it was a place where we could all just be. It's where I saw Madiba and Mrs Machel truly happy and enjoying life to the fullest. (Mrs Machel retained the surname to honour her first husband, former Mozambiquan president Samora Machel, who died in a plane crash in 1986, believed to have been orchestrated by the apartheid regime. In private, I called her Mum.) Time is so fleeting, yet we never imagined it would end because in those moments we could float, carefree, without thinking about the future – or the past, for that matter. You never had to watch your words because the intention was known. You never had to feel ashamed of your body because the acceptance was so complete. I'll never forget the pure joy I saw on Madiba's face when we set a plastic chair for him in the shallow waves so he could enjoy the water breaking over his feet. The joy that fills my heart from such memories is precious, and I sometimes fear that, as time passes, these memories will fade until they become unrecognisable even to me.

Haruki Murakami, in *Kafka on the Shore*, writes: 'Memories warm you up from the inside. But they also tear you apart.' You never get used to the loss of a loved one and, even though Madiba was not a blood relative, my life had revolved around him. He made me who I am, and I felt lost without him. Suddenly I had no purpose and faced the challenge of having to create one. Writing *Good Morning, Mr Mandela* so soon after Madiba's death, and then embarking on a public speaking career that honoured his legacy, shielded me from the real grieving process I should have gone through.

When I think about the path I've chosen, I ask myself: would I ever be able to work for someone else again? I doubt it. It would be unfair to another person to expect them to be like Madiba, and it would be equally unfair to expect me to dedicate myself to a new person in a working environment in that way.

Even today, I'm often stopped in the street when people feel the urge to talk to me about Madiba. It's quite amusing how my persona has changed in people's minds over the years. First I was Zelda of Madiba, then I became Zelda with the motorbike (more about this later) and then Zelda who wrote the book. For many people, the idea of me was better than the reality of me. I hadn't become the person they wanted me to be. I was too strong, talked too much, commented too easily and often spoke my mind. Every person had a different expectation of what I should be, how I should act and behave, and how I should deal with my past.

Lately I am stopped or contacted at least a few times a week by people who have Nelson Mandela memorabilia that they want to sell or donate to me. I sometimes feel like the curator of a museum. But people's urge to relate their Madiba stories to me has remained constant. Although I appreciated that I was the extension or connection they yearned for after his death, I also needed time and space to come to terms with the nineteen years that had happened to me. I had to create distance so I could reflect on the unprecedented privilege I'd had of knowing and loving Madiba. What was next for me?

In addition to mourning the loss of Madiba – to the degree I allowed myself – I didn't realise at the time that I was also mourning the loss of South Africa as we knew it. The country of possibility and dreams, of overcoming adversity, was slowly slipping away. ANC members who have since left the party, as well as South Africans across the political spectrum, feel deceived. The ANC abandoned an entire country and its beautiful people to poverty, crime, corruption and mismanagement. But it's not only South Africa that feels the pain. There's a worldwide shift away from democracy. I often ask myself how we got here.

Personally, I was living like a hovercraft, with nothing to ground me. Not dealing with the reality of grief meant that I had to take control of the situation 'after Madiba' – which, to me, meant that I had to defend him and his legacy. Unfortunately, this came with a smouldering anger fanned by my own inability to deal with grief.

I had no consideration or respect for grief until my lowest point during the Twitter storm, when I was brought back to earth with a bump. As much as the question irritated me, I finally had to face the hard task of asking myself what I'd learnt.

During my public speaking, I tell the story of apartheid and how I was part of the system based on superiority. I recall my first meeting with Madiba and how that experience moved me to confront my past. But have I really understood what that meant? I share lessons learnt about respect, compassion, integrity and ethics. But have I fully embodied these lessons? Can I truly say that I live by conviction, not convenience?

What others have found helpful over the past ten years is my brutal honesty when it comes to storytelling. Many people shy away from personal storytelling because they're afraid of exposing themselves, their flaws and their shortcomings. I've learnt to speak about my mistakes and struggles so that others, too, may find the courage to do so. We can only learn from each other if we share our personal stories, whether good or bad. No one is ever exclusively good or bad. Our struggles and hardships are universal. Learning from our own mistakes is helpful and wise. Learning from the mistakes of others is quicker, easier and less expensive.

The world is a different place from what Madiba left behind. These ten years have felt like a lifetime but also like the blink of an eye. The changes are immense: the world as we know it now is unforgiving, and egotists rule some of the most powerful corporates and nations across the globe.

On 5 February 1999, Madiba addressed Parliament for the last time before his retirement in May that year. He said, 'We slaughter one another in our words and attitudes. We slaughter one another in the stereotypes and mistrust that linger in our heads, and the words of hate we spew from our lips.'

I, like everyone else, often wonder what he would have said or done had he been alive today. The sensible moderates have gone into hiding. The world is dominated by violence, hate and vengeance, and we all ask: where are our leaders? The behaviour of the left is pushing idealistic realists – those who see the world as it is but have a vision of what it could be – towards the right, and I find myself questioning my beliefs because of it. People are not giving each other permission to learn. The brutality of our judgement of others is the norm.

South Africa is a land of vast contrasts. One day we celebrate someone's victory or success and bask in euphoria, and the next we find ourselves in the valley of despair. But we are a resolute people, and I know we can overcome whatever challenges we now face.

I still often ask myself: what exactly was it about Madiba that inspired so many people across the world? One thing of which I'm certain is that he gave us all the courage to be better. He reflected only the best in us so that we could see what was humanly possible. It was easy to love him, even if you'd never met him. He gave us the strength and courage not to change those around us but to change ourselves.

Sadly, that influence is gone now. His successor, Thabo Mbeki, set us on a path of economic renewal. Thank goodness he did, as it protected us, to some extent, from the effects of the 2008 financial crisis in the US. But it came at a price. The agenda of reconciliation, unity and non-racialism was moved to the back burner and gave way to populists using insults and vulgarity as a substitute for wit. Now, 30 years after the dawn of democracy, the gap between our reality and what we thought it would be is greater than ever.

Personally, I've been on a rollercoaster ride over the past decade. The first couple of months after Madiba's passing were hard. A sadness engulfed me when I realised that it was finally over and the person I'd known, loved and dedicated my life to was gone.

On many occasions, and indeed in many areas of my life, I've battled with decision-making. In this, as in so many other ways, I feel lost without Madiba – I miss his sound advice. But from time to time, signs appear. While filming the six-part 2018 documentary series *A Glorious Human Achievement: Nelson Mandela*, we interviewed one of Madiba's fellow Robben Island inmates, Eddie Daniels. The series was about the people and places that had influenced Nelson Mandela. It was a meaningful journey that took us on a tour across the country as we reconnected with his legacy and delved into history.

Having been tried and sentenced for sabotage activities, Oom (Uncle) Eddie served his term on Robben Island and was put in the same section as Madiba, even though he was a member of the Liberal Party at the time, not the ANC. They spent fifteen years in prison together, and Oom Eddie was always a joy to receive when he visited Madiba after their release. The purpose of our interviews was to record as many memories as possible from the people who'd known Madiba in prison. Having arranged with Oom Eddie's family and staff at the retirement home where he was in frail care, we went to see him. He was keen to contribute and insisted on being let out of the frail-care unit to do the interview in his home in the retirement village. The place had obviously been closed for some time and it was stuffy inside, so we opened some doors and windows while setting up for the interview.

As well as sharing a wealth of information about their time in prison, Oom Eddie didn't hold back on the emotional side. As we concluded the interview, I asked (my voice cracking with emotion): 'Oom Eddie, do you miss Madiba?' He was silent for a while. It was a still, windless day, yet in that moment the wind chimes hanging in the doorway started tinkling. The crew members and I looked up, surprised. But we didn't want to interrupt the moment as Oom Eddie whispered, 'I miss him very much. Very much.' I don't believe in numerology, nor do I believe in ghosts or the supernatural. I do, however, think that sometimes those who have passed on communicate with us in ways that transcend our understanding of communication. A few months after our interview, Oom Eddie passed away.

As I was contemplating this book and struggling to put pen to paper, I was at the Mount Nelson hotel in Cape Town for a speaking engagement, waiting for the audience to arrive. I rely on public-speaking engagements, and for that I need an audience and people to gather or travel. When the Covid-19 restrictions in South Africa were announced on 15 March 2020, I lost six months' worth of work in an instant; my diary looked as if the rapture had happened. As a result, I used my pension money to stay afloat. The Mount Nelson engagement was the first after a long work drought. I had a few minutes to myself and thought of the privilege of being able to work again, to have an audience and people willing to listen to my story. Should I write another book, I wondered? Immersed in the moment, I heard one of the doors leading from the garden into the ballroom open. I prepared to greet people with a smile, but when I turned around, I saw that the door had opened by itself. It had clear glass windowpanes, and I could see that there was no one outside who could have opened it and there was not a breath of wind. It sent shivers down my spine, and I took it as an affirmation. I'm not done yet. I still have much to learn and to say.

As I mentioned, making decisions is often challenging. It's hard being a single, middle-aged woman without direction and purpose, when I was once consumed by someone else's life. I've made some terribly expensive travel mistakes, and I've realised it's easier to organise someone else's life than my own. While having endless debates with myself about decisions, Madiba's birth date, his prison number or versions thereof, have appeared on the cash receipt as I've mindlessly bought a cup of coffee, or as the room number assigned to me in a hotel. I guess if you're open to it, you'll see these things as meaningful, as signs, but I believe that sometimes the affirmation we need is found in nature and the world around us.

While still trying to cling to Madiba and his influence in my life, two of his closest friends, Ahmed Kathrada and George Bizos, passed away. I'd remained close to both: they were always willing to offer support and advice and to reminisce with me. Kathy, as we fondly called Mr Kathrada, eagerly shared anecdotes about Madiba in prison and how difficult he'd made it for warders by questioning every letter of every sentence they uttered – a side of Madiba people conveniently forget today. Uncle George often retold the stories of the different trials

Madiba had been involved in over the years and how they'd argued cases by simply stating the obvious facts. People were not always prepared to hear the truth, but the two of them fed off each other's quest for truth and righteousness. I found it comforting that I only had to look at these two men's lives to be reminded how to emulate the essence of Madiba. Their principles unequivocally aligned with his. Their focus, right until the end of their days, was the pursuit of what was just, even – perhaps especially – in our battered society. This gave me the insight that living according to and embodying Madiba's principles was the way to keep his influence and legacy alive – not just for me but for others, too.

In March 2017, when Kathy died, I attended his funeral with Madiba's wife, Graça Machel. Kathy had been at odds with then President Zuma for several years, criticising him on many occasions. By now, most of the ANC stalwarts had spoken about corruption and mismanagement under Zuma's leadership. The funeral was marked by political comments, and it was a watershed moment in South Africa when those with integrity took a clear stand against corruption. The president didn't attend the funeral – 'in accordance with the family's wishes', he said at the time. But it's likely he realised that – just as Kathy's own comments had been all his life – most of the tributes would be politically loaded. I was proud to be there on that day, which was one of the last occasions Mrs Machel, Madiba's grandson Mandla Mandela, Uncle George Bizos and I were together at the same venue. Madiba's presence was slowly slipping away, and his absence was felt by all.

During the Covid-19 pandemic, in September 2020, Uncle George passed away. He'd practised as an advocate and was part of the team that defended Madiba and his co-accused during the Rivonia Trial in 1963–64. This time I could not attend the funeral, as travel restrictions were in place. But I really wanted to honour him for the life he'd led, for what he'd done and for his remarkable 67-year friendship with Madiba. So, I issued a statement to the media that began by referring to the dedication at the front of his book *Odyssey to Freedom*: 'For those who let me walk with them', because that definitely included Madiba.

I continued: 'Uncle George walked the road with Madiba during the toughest times of his life. A beacon of strength and character for the 67 years of their friendship. Someone that literally kept him upright by reciting the law to remind Madiba that he was on the road of righteousness.'

I said he had embodied the definition of ethics – what was good for the self and the other.

'The humility, simplicity, absence of vanity and generosity of spirit that Nelson Mandela greatly admired in people were qualities easily detected in George Bizos', whose life calling and passion were to 'defend anyone ill-treated or disadvantaged'.

My statement ended with these words: 'Although I am sad tonight, I know he joined the illustrious company of people at peace with themselves and the world. I loved him deeply, but I know his separation from his friend "Nelson", as he called him, is finally over. They were like shooting stars through whom we saw a glimpse of consonance. They illuminated our world and now they are gone.'

Although Covid caused immense suffering for people worldwide, it was also a time for us to reflect. I realised during that period that we are never completely changed. We change in phases, and we only stop changing the day we die. We should therefore not look at a person at any one point in their life to establish whether they've changed, but rather keep nudging them in the right direction.

I never thought I'd say this, but although I lost some work as a result, I'm grateful for my dreadful Twitter experience and what I learnt from it.

In addition to the real people who got down and dirty in the mud-slinging match that followed my tweets in 2015, it's likely that I naively engaged with anonymous trolls who were invading the Twitterscape and voicing anger and hatred without consequence. At the time, we didn't know that a much bigger strategy was taking shape. Although there's no proof that British PR, reputation management and marketing company Bell Pottinger was involved in my ordeal, the overall plan was clearly already in place. We know today that 'paid Twitter' played a huge part in fomenting dissent and inflaming racial tensions in South Africa through comments planted by this company. Investigations revealed that Zuma's people forked out large amounts of money for this Machiavellian strategy, designed to 'divide and rule'. Ironically, it was not much different from the apartheid regime's modus operandi. Divide and rule. Sow division and cause distraction while the large-scale looting of public resources continues unabated.

Getting back to my Twitter lesson: I learnt that compassion, respect, humility, sincerity, kindness and ethics are fundamentally part of our characters but also of leadership.

I can be a kind person and still say no, prioritise my needs, set boundaries and disagree with people. I can be kind even when I challenge poor behaviour or stand up for myself and walk away from toxic environments – even when I make mistakes. I can walk away from cruelty without the need to detonate a mini atom bomb. But how? It's something I ponder daily as situations crop up and I'm challenged or cornered in some way.

This book is not a self-help guide to leadership but rather an anecdotal account of how Madiba's impact on my life has manifested itself. The leadership themes can be considered a tool to let us return to the value-based leadership we yearn for in modern society. We can't change others; we can only change ourselves, as Madiba taught us. Now, more than ever, we need people who exhibit a higher form of self-awareness to do the introspection, just as Madiba did.

Ten years after his passing, I feel that I've gained clarity about the effect Madiba had on my life. My vision is clear as I tread carefully in the footsteps of one of the greatest leaders of our time.

I can't blame you if you can't forgive me. I struggle to forgive myself. But I've realised an act doesn't have to be forgiven for you to learn from it. My duty is to learn from my mistakes. However, I had to root out the obnoxious weeds of self-flagellation so I could fulfil my purpose, which is to share my experiences and my insights into the man I knew so well. I've written about some of the stories before, but in life some things bear repeating.

After making many mistakes and seeing how these affected my psyche, I've learnt to find equanimity. Yes, I'm angry, but so is everyone else. We need to manage that anger and not lose focus about the direction we want for our communities and our country. What do you want to be known for? Being an angry, bitter person who can't adapt to change, or someone who is willing to give up a little for the sake of the greater good?

We should all do things we know we can do. Give your thoughts wings and interrogate your cognitive bias. The thing is, everyone belongs. It is what made Madiba so loved. He made us all belong. Even in his travels across the globe, through individuals' interaction with him, he made them feel they belonged, no matter who or where they were. By displaying sincerity and dignity, we can establish resonance with each other.

A narcissist doesn't go to a psychiatrist, and psychopaths are convinced there's nothing wrong with them. To be in denial or to put our heads in the sand and pretend that nothing is broken in society is equally catastrophic. We need to be brutally honest with ourselves.

If we truly admire Madiba, what can we do to give meaning to his legacy and to live a life that honours him? It's not only up to the people who knew him. Many of us were first-hand witnesses to the remarkable story of Nelson Mandela and his leadership in action. Unless we all insist on the values and morals that he lived his life by, people will distort his legacy and detract from what he achieved.

We're all familiar with how words and events can be manipulated to suit a particular agenda. Similarly, if someone repeatedly tells a lie, it becomes believable to the person telling it, and in time they can no longer distinguish between the lie and the truth. I'm so aware that we should guard against this happening with Madiba's true story. Even the Bible, considered to be a sacred text, was used during apartheid to convince white people that they were the chosen ones, superior in every way. Over the centuries, people have attributed different meanings to parts of the Bible, to such an extent that it's at risk of being regarded as a fable. In no way am I trying to compare the Bible to the story of Madiba. The point is that if we don't write and talk about his legacy as often as possible, it'll be given new interpretations by those who come after us, diluting the truth that his life showed how good could triumph over evil.

We must avoid being overwhelmed by the suffering and injustice the world dishes out daily and work together to create a different, more equitable reality – as Madiba tried to do. Many people have told me over the years that I don't have to defend his legacy. I disagree. We need to refute claims that Madiba was a sell-out, that he compromised too much or that he was weak and didn't do enough to advance black people in South Africa. We need to tell stories that reflect the reality of his life.

How do we overcome the distrust among us? Once, Madiba freed us from that distrust. I believe it's important for us to interrogate how he did it. When people meet me, they like to bemoan the state of our nation. It's a lot to bear, and the negativity gets to me. Being a chronic defeatist is middle-class and comes from a point of privilege. Millions of people live in severe poverty in our country, and even if they feel defeated, they get up every day and hustle to make ends meet despite the overwhelming challenges they face. Today, the work done by non-profit and non-governmental organisations keeps this country going. Most people aren't willing to get their hands dirty. We plead poverty.

But when it doesn't cost you much and it can mean something to someone, whatever the size of your contribution, you should just do it.

In the closing paragraphs of Madiba's biography, *Long Walk to Freedom*, he wrote:

> I have walked that long road to freedom. I have tried not to falter; I have made missteps along the way. But I have discovered the secret that after climbing a great hill, one only finds that there are many more hills to climb. I have taken a moment here to rest, to steal a view of the glorious vista that surrounds me, to look back on the distance I have come. But I can rest only for a moment, for with freedom come responsibilities, and I dare not linger, for my long walk is not ended.

Despite my missteps, my journey has not ended either. I have much to learn and much to contribute. I share my story and experiences because I want others to learn from my mistakes too, just as I continue to learn from the lessons of my time with Madiba.

During the Twitter ordeal, there were many things I should have remembered, things I'd learnt from Madiba. The first is never to respond when you're angry. South Africa went through a particularly hard time during the 'lost years' of Zuma's presidency, a period of great uncertainty in our history. As a country, we'd forgotten what we'd learnt from Madiba; I, too, did not remember many things.

Another important lesson that I wish I had recalled during my Twitter ordeal is: you'll never do anything in your life that will please everyone. That rotten situation presented the perfect compost to grow the opposition against me. Some people felt that I wasn't worthy of a share in Madiba's life. I simply didn't suit their narrative. Perhaps they thought that I tended to whitewash Madiba's history, seeing only the good in him. But seeing the best in others characterised Madiba himself, and he was all too aware of it. In *Conversations with Myself*, comprising letters Madiba wrote from prison, he said, 'People will feel I see too much good in people. So, it's a criticism I have to put up with and I've tried to adjust to because whether it is so or not, it is something which I think is profitable. It's a good thing to assume, to act on the basis that others are men of integrity and honour because you tend to attract integrity and honour if that is how you regard those with whom you work.'

In a professional capacity, I'm the person who spent the most time with Madiba after his release from prison. It wasn't hours, days or weeks, but years. People have the notion that I was infatuated by him in a sense. But it's not true. There were many moments of anger, disapproval and indifference.

I fully appreciate that there's intense jealousy that I had the extra-ordinary opportunity to spend so much time with him. I understand that people feel I didn't deserve it. But I can't defend his choices and decisions. For the first four years I was in a job I'd applied for. Then I was promoted and, effectively for the remaining fifteen years, he chose me to be at his side to carry out his wishes.

I never believed that my career with him was anything but a privilege – the greatest honour one could imagine. People ask whether I feel I sacrificed anything, and I always say no. It's a genuine answer, but I also acknowledge the reality that while people my age were dating, getting married and having children, I was working day and night. I have no regrets, but in the moments when I reflect on the harsh criticism that's been aimed at me over the years, I wonder if I should have been a bit more selfish. This is just a fleeting thought, though, because I know, in my bones, that my commitment and focus were complete. I'm not saying I was right or that I have life – particularly my own – all figured out.

I learn. Every. Single. Day.

PART II

Timeless lessons

Every drop counts

What counts in life is not the mere fact that we have lived.
It is what difference we have made to the lives of others that
will determine the significance of the life we lead.

– Said at the 90th birthday celebration of Walter Sisulu, 18 May 2002,
from the Nelson Mandela Foundation archives

Hindsight is a wonderful thing. You imagine what you could or should have done in the face of disaster, and the result plays out differently in your head even as the reality remains like an ink stain on a white linen shirt. It fades but remains with you every day to remind you of the host of possibilities if you'd acted differently.

A friend and wise professor from North-West University told me that the Twitter ordeal would remain with me for at least two years. The memory was so painful that I wanted it obliterated from my mind. But it took much, much longer for me to reflect on it. I retreated from the public space for a long time to face what I'd done. I should not have reacted impulsively. I should have focused on the task at hand and not been side-tracked, no matter how politically invested I felt in South Africa. I should have taken the time, as Madiba taught me, to think before reacting. While I now know what I should not have done, it is also true that many of the lessons he taught me stuck with me subconsciously and helped me a great deal to reflect and move forward.

But the pertinent question about what I'd learnt remained: how do you measure impact? Is it by quantity, consistency or frequency, or can it be measured by attitude?

On 19 December 2013, a fortnight after Madiba's passing, I was at a birthday luncheon at insurance mogul Douw Steyn's home. Douw had been introduced to Madiba by Thabo Mbeki and Oliver Tambo after a meeting in Lusaka before the ANC was unbanned. My eyes were bloodshot from constant crying over the previous two weeks, and a feeling of exhaustion and overwhelming sadness enveloped me. I desperately needed to sleep for a long and uninterrupted period, and I was fighting the fatigue with every breath I took. No matter which of his lovely residences I was invited to, Douw had always offered an oasis of tranquillity where I could feel at home under any circumstances.

There was nothing to celebrate, but one of the things Mrs Machel taught me was that if anyone wanted to honour Madiba, they should honour his relationships with people. I thought it was therefore important to be at Douw's birthday lunch, a small gathering of not more than fifteen people. Douw, not well himself at that point, was feeling the sadness as we huddled around the table.

When someone close to you dies, you try to avoid talking about anything that could take you back to the subject. You force your thoughts and feelings to focus on something else because you know you have to get through at least an hour or so without crying again. Small victories.

To try to lift the mood, Douw's wife, Carolyn, and his long-time right-hand man, Jonathan, told me that they'd engaged in a swimming contest. They'd been daring each other to take on different things, and Jonathan had won the swim-off.

My thoughts flipped through a few ideas as I tried to find something I knew Carolyn could beat him at. Out loud, I said, 'How about baking?' – knowing very well that when it came to domestic chores, Carolyn and I were on a par with each other. We can't boil water without burning it. To the amusement of the other guests, we quickly moved on from that suggestion. I knew I had to find something unique to her. 'How about you crochet a blanket?' I suggested. I'd seen her crochet once or twice and, associating this pastime with a much older person, asked her about it. She'd said it was therapeutic.

There was silence around the table. I could see my suggestion was gaining traction. Jonathan smiled; I suspected he couldn't pick up a stitch even if his life depended on it. No judgement – it's not as if I can. While the guests were still laughing about my suggestion, Carolyn said she'd take on the challenge if Jonathan did. I chipped in again: 'Even better, why don't you crochet 67 blankets for Madiba's birthday on 18 July next year? 67 blankets for Mandela Day.' The number 67 symbolises the number of years Madiba fought for human rights and the abolition of apartheid since he became politically active in 1942.

Less than a week later, Carolyn's sister Sharon arrived at their Christmas lunch with needles and wool for Carolyn to start her blanket. She was up for the challenge but knew she'd need a little help to crochet 67 blankets. She wasted no time, and in January 2014, she officially established the 67 Blankets for Nelson Mandela Day initiative. In January 2024, I celebrated the initiative's tenth anniversary with them. Thousands of blankets have been made across the globe, and the initiative holds the Guinness World Record for the largest crocheted blanket in the world, measuring 3 377 square metres. Most importantly, these blankets have touched and warmed the hearts of hundreds of thousands of people. The initiative has taken on a life of its own and given people purpose. Every week and on almost every continent, people gather in groups to sit together and knit or crochet in the name of Nelson Mandela. It's so much more than providing warmth for those in need during winter. It also creates a sense of belonging among people who may otherwise not be part of any meaningful project that brings about change.

I could never have imagined that a simple idea being bandied about over lunch could have such a profound impact – one that's grown way beyond our borders. Of course, had it not been for Carolyn pursuing the idea with her special verve and energy, it may well have been just another noble yet short-lived initiative. I saw Madiba believing that if he touched just one person's life every day, he could change the world – and we know that he achieved exactly that. The blanket initiative emulates that ideal. We have the power to change other people's destinies, not just our own.

I had organised seven Bikers for Mandela Day initiatives between 2010 and 2016, during which a group of motorbike enthusiasts would travel to a remote rural area to help some of the most impoverished people in our country. The bikers would dedicate their time and effort to bringing about change in communities by rebuilding homes, fixing roofs, planting vegetable gardens and renovating safe houses to help restore the dignity of women who were survivors of gender-based violence. The programme also branched out to neighbouring countries, and the most touching case for me was when we supported a woman in Botswana who had been disfigured when her South African lover poured boiling oil over her face and body. She had children to support, but she couldn't find employment because of her appearance. We fixed up her house and established a vegetable garden to help her feed her family. And no, this did not solve all her problems, but we did something and touched her life.

Many people adopted the model and created like-minded groups as far afield as India. Sadly, I had to disengage myself from the initiative because not all participants shared the seriousness and accountability of engaging in a project carrying the Mandela name. The responsibility became too much to bear for our core group of organisers. I hold dear the memories of this initiative, the friendships I formed and the cumulative power of people reaching out. As mentioned earlier it was because of this initiative that people starting referring to me as 'Zelda with the bike'.

After moving to my new home in the Western Cape in 2018, I became involved with a home for orphans and vulnerable children in the region. South Africa's orphans and vulnerable children are in desperate need of dedicated care and attention. Many of these children are taken in by non-governmental organisations that run homes for them, and they do a magnificent job at providing critical care: basic needs such as food, clothing and safety. However, once children enter these homes, they stop dreaming. In an average household, we take for granted that children get the undivided attention of a parent, as well as guidance, advice, exposure and life support in general. A house mother taking care of twelve to twenty children can't offer more than the basics to her charges in terms of career advice and planning. For many children, the end of a stable family life also means the end of possibility and progress. It's a mammoth task but something I wish to influence. Through a pilot project, we aim to provide career advice and aptitude tests by using volunteers in the community to offer their skills and knowledge. Through the intervention of friends and family, I try to create social opportunities for the kids that expose them to broader experiences and a wider range of people – one thing I never took for granted during my time with Madiba. Such exposure changed the trajectory of my life path, and I wish to share that with others.

When I'm asked what I learnt from Madiba, I can offer anecdotal accounts of the lessons I learnt, but something that can't be quantified is the urgency I feel in seeking opportunities to help others, no matter my personal circumstances.

This is what we had in mind when we approached the South African ambassador to the United Nations (UN), Dumisani Khumalo, and his deputy, Baso Sangqu, to help us lobby the UN to declare 18 July Nelson Mandela International Day. 'We' refers to me, 46664 international director Tim Massey and concert promoter Roddy Quinn, as well as Achmat Dangor, CEO of the Nelson Mandela Foundation, with the backing of foundation chair Prof Jakes Gerwel. You may not be able to measure impact or count the number of people affected, and you may never know the effort and time it cost the people who are involved, but it will inspire change. If this change begins with an individual action, then we will all have succeeded. Every deed in the right direction counts.

For me, the first step to understanding Madiba is acknowledging that he was a human being with vices and virtues, like all of us. For anyone to imply that you must have learnt to be sanctimonious or flawless because you worked for Nelson Mandela would be to deny the very humanity that Madiba taught us to respect in each other.

Madiba was a realist: he knew the difficulties of creating a just and equal society, and of people learning to live together and respect one another, given our past. But he would be deeply concerned that people's dignity is not being honoured and respected 30 years after the dawn of democracy. He knew that improvements were possible. People talk about 'the dream' Nelson Mandela had, but we saw during his time in office that it wasn't just a dream. It became reality.

There's a limit to what one can do if people themselves are limited: the education system in our country continues to fail our children, and they grow up believing that only the worst in their lives is possible. But even if there's political turmoil and discord, we as ordinary people can try to do better by getting involved in community service. People who claim to feel helpless often ask me what they can do. If you simply look beyond the needs of your immediate household, there are endless opportunities to be of service and make a meaningful contribution to someone else's life. For example, if you're bringing up children of your own or are a retired teacher, you could take a child from an underprivileged area under your wing and help them with homework. The vast gap between rich and poor in our country is growing wider every day, pulling it apart at the seams; we need to stitch it back together through civil society. Thousands of people dedicate their lives to philanthropy – being of service to others – and it inspires others to participate too.

When I dedicate time to helping others, I find a deeper connection to Madiba. He was always looking for opportunities to help those in need. When he read horrific stories in newspapers about people going through a crisis, it was never too much trouble to find those individuals and make a telephone call to express his support or condolences to those who were suffering. Occasionally, if he couldn't help personally, he would connect people to those who had the means to do so. It's impossible to help everyone, but you must do what you can. It all adds up. Every drop counts.

It's often in the small acts, such as reaching out to the injured or offering unsolicited kindness to strangers, where Madiba had the biggest influence on my life.

A few years ago, I read in the newspaper about a young farmer in one of the northern provinces of South Africa who was the victim of a farm attack. He was recovering in hospital but was heartbroken about his Boston terrier that had been brutally killed – hanged – in front of him while he was powerless to stop it happening. I couldn't bear his pain and sent him flowers in hospital to sympathise with the death of his beloved best friend. I've had a few Boston terriers in my life. They become part of your family because of their almost-human nature. The flowers were delivered by a reliable service, so I'm sure he received them. I didn't hear from him and didn't expect to, but I hoped that my gesture had showed him that someone, somewhere, thought of him and felt his pain.

When the popular Afrikaans singer Theuns Jordaan died of cancer in November 2021, it was a huge shock to his fans and everyone who knew him personally. I'd met Theuns on a few occasions and, when I arranged a variety performance to take place at our Johannesburg office, I asked him to be among the artists invited to entertain Madiba with their music and art. As Theuns and I had only encountered one another at events, he was an acquaintance rather than a friend. Nonetheless, I'd asked mutual friends and some of his fellow artists to keep me posted about his battle with cancer. I also knew that his mother was quite ill, and I heard that Theuns' death at the age of just 50 had shocked her deeply. She passed away barely two weeks later.

I managed to get his sister's contact details and extended my condolences to her and her father, Oom Willie. On Christmas Day, just over a month after Theuns' death, I decided to call his dad. I'm never overly excited about Christmas – perhaps because we don't have small children in our family and therefore don't really make a big fuss over it. It irks me that people tend to gather in small groups, usually exclusively with family, and exclude others who may not celebrate Christmas or who are alone. I also hate the excessiveness of Christmas, whether it's food or gifts being exchanged, while for so many people, Christmas is just another day of hunger and poverty. Madiba insisted every year that we organise a Christmas party for children in need in the rural Eastern Cape, and he would always be there to greet them. This made me even more aware of how my own experience of Christmas, especially while growing up, was incredibly privileged and selfish.

I can't imagine how devastating it must be to a family who have just lost a wife, mother, son or brother, to have to 'celebrate' Christmas. So, I reached out to Oom Willie. I'd met him and his wife once at an Afrikaans festival where Theuns was performing, but I didn't expect him to remember me. I knew Theuns' mother had read my first book and loved it; she'd told me so when we met.

Today, I thought, on this Christmas Day, rather than looking at presents under the nonexistent tree, I should do something for someone else. I'd long forgotten how meaningful and rewarding Christmas had been to me when I'd worked with Madiba on the day, bringing joy to others. I picked up the phone and had an hour-long conversation with Oom Willie. We cried and we laughed – two strangers just passing the time on that dreaded day. I called him a few times thereafter to ask about his wellbeing. It made me feel close to Madiba again because I knew this was the sort of thing he'd done so effortlessly every day: just reaching out to someone in need, sharing his time. That is his lasting impact on me.

Seeing everyone in the room

Bridge the chasm, use tolerance and compassion, be inclusive not exclusive, build dignity and pride, encourage freedom of expression to create a civil society for unity and peace.

– *Nelson Mandela by Himself: The Authorised Book of Quotations*, p 225

What Madiba did best was to accept people exactly as they were, in their totality. He worked with people who were willing to change, knowing that if you believed in someone, it didn't mean that person would never make a mistake.

In a transcribed conversation with author Richard Stengel, who collaborated with Madiba on the writing of his autobiography, *Long Walk to Freedom*, Madiba said:

Your duty is to work with human beings as human beings, not because you think they are angels. And therefore, once you know that this man has got this virtue and he has got this weakness, you work with them and you accommodate that weakness and you try and help him to overcome that weakness. I don't want to be frightened by the fact that a person has made a certain mistake, and he has got human frailties. I cannot allow myself to be influenced by that.

I've often been criticised for associating with people from all walks of life – people who may feel and think differently. However, the one thing I can't do is build friendships with blatant racists. If I can work on myself continuously to undo the prejudice and bias I was exposed to for much of my young life, there should be no excuse for anyone else to hold on to those things either. I acknowledge that I was able to change much sooner than my peers because of the exposure I had through my job. But now, 30 years after democracy, I can't operate in an environment where people hold on to the past. You have to want to try, at least.

In his Nobel Peace Prize acceptance speech at the award ceremony in Norway on 10 December 1993, Madiba said, 'Thus shall we live, because we will have created a society which recognises that all people are born equal, with each entitled in equal measure to life, liberty, prosperity, human rights and good governance.'

Inspired by this, I always consider equal ground to be my starting point with people. Having worked and interacted for many years with highly qualified people who have achieved great things, I've come to understand a bit about human nature. When Stephen Hawking, arguably the world's most famous scientist, met Madiba during his 2008 visit to South Africa to launch the Next Einstein initiative, designed to discover and nurture maths and science talent in Africa, he didn't project himself as Madiba's superior. Beyoncé and Bono didn't use their megastar status to outshine Madiba when they appeared with him, and some of the wealthiest people on this planet never felt the need to tell Madiba about their riches or status. Even Queen Elizabeth and Madiba were on first-name terms. I tell myself that when people on that level can relate as ordinary human beings, I should never consider myself anything but equal during an encounter with another person. I sometimes slip, but then I remind myself how many of the highly educated, wealthy and famous people that I met always treated me as an equal.

Yet, in my small world, I often come across individuals who behave as if they have some advantage over others. They want to dazzle you with their wealth, qualifications, achievements, status or position, or they claim that their race or religion is superior to that of another. Having sat with people who were dying, it became clear to me that in that raw edge between life and death, none of what you've accumulated or achieved matters. As humanity was a core principle for Madiba, one that guided and informed his actions, he made a point of truly 'seeing' and thus acknowledging individuals. He was exceptional at treating people with dignity, irrespective of their standing in life.

I've been a regular speaker at Young Presidents' Organization gatherings in recent years. There are various membership requirements, including that you have to be under the age of 45 and the head of an organisation. The figure your company needs to generate varies according to different fields, but annual employee compensation must exceed $2,5 million. Most members are dollar millionaires before the age of 30, so many of the members I've met over the years are incredibly successful. Yet, like Madiba, they have the grace and poise to 'see' every individual in the room as special in their own right. You don't hear them bad-mouthing others, they don't spend time discussing people and they'll always find a way to compliment someone.

As a result of their mindset, successful people tend to exude positive energy. You could argue that you'd also be a nice person if you had the same bank balance, but most of these individuals were precisely who they are today way before they became successful businesspeople. They usually come from humble beginnings and applied hard work and complete commitment to become who they are. None of them ever told me that they'd always been successful or rich. It starts with a humble and simple story, and they show character and principle in success.

I came across a wonderful tale that reflects a practical application of these words and reminds me how Madiba treated people when they were at their most vulnerable.

An old man meets a young man who asks: 'Do you remember me?'

The old man says no. The young man tells him he was his student, and that, inspired by his example, he became a teacher. Curious, the old man asks when he decided to become a teacher. The young man replies: 'One day a friend of mine came to school with a nice new watch and I decided I wanted it. So, I stole it. When my friend noticed his watch was missing, he complained to our teacher, who was you. You addressed the class, saying the watch had been stolen and that whoever stole it should please return it. I didn't give it back because I didn't want to.

'You closed the door and told us to stand up and form a circle. You were going to search our pockets one by one until the watch was found. However, you told us to close our eyes because you would only look for the watch if we all had our eyes closed. When you went through my pockets, you found the watch and took it. You kept searching everyone's pockets, and when you were done, you said, "Open your eyes. We have the watch."

'You didn't tell on me, and you never mentioned the episode. You never said who stole the watch either. It was the most shameful day of my life. But this is also the day I decided not to become a thief or a bad person, because you saved my dignity. You never said anything, nor did you even scold me or take me aside to give me a moral lesson. I received your message clearly. Thanks to you, I understood what a real educator needs to do. Do you remember this episode?'

The old man answered, 'Yes, I remember the situation. But I didn't remember you because I also closed my eyes while looking.'

This is the essence of teaching. If to correct you must humiliate, you don't know how to teach.

When I heard this story, I could identify so well with the character of the teacher. To me, Madiba was that teacher: always eager to share his teaching without ever having to humiliate anyone in the process. Sadly, humiliation has become part of everyday life. I don't think it comes naturally to us to turn the other cheek in response to being humiliated. And, with social media playing such a big part in our lives, it's easy for 'the enemy' to be in your face all the time. When someone has humiliated you, you want to take revenge when the Ferris wheel turns and the opportunity presents itself for you to be on the righteous side. But from Madiba's life we can learn that when the enemy acts without conscience, we must resist the temptation to do the same. The way you show compassion to those who may have wronged you enriches your character. Given the terrible crime statistics in South Africa, we're often exposed to interviews with victims' families. Their pain and anguish make people feel that the perpetrators deserve the harshest sentence. I have to work hard to stop myself from sharing their feelings. I think: who appointed me to judge another person's wrongdoing? Archbishop Desmond Tutu and Madiba believed that even the most hardened criminal deserved compassion.

Perhaps the following example doesn't fall into the 'hardened criminal' league, but it's a situation I can at least bring myself to mull over: what would I do if I had no means to feed my hungry children? Difficult as it is to confess, I think I have it in me to turn to crime if I was out of other options. This makes me realise that before judging others, I should put myself in their shoes. You never know how a situation will affect you until you're in it. Desperation might drive me to the same deed. I'm by no means trying to justify breaking the law, under any circumstances, but perhaps trying to understand how poverty affects the social conscience.

The majority of middle-class folks, including me, don't understand the depths of despair that can result from severe poverty. One story – among countless in our country – brought it home for me in a powerful, albeit distressing, way. A friend and popular South African DJ and radio presenter invited listeners of his show to share their problems so he could try to support them where possible. A man called in to say he was unemployed and had three children to feed. The children sometimes cried nonstop at night, purely from hunger. He realised the children had learnt that when he boiled water on the gas burner, it was usually to prepare food. So, even when there was no food, he would boil water to soothe the children as they fell asleep crying, because they imagined that there was food on the way.

The story broke me. I cried for days and asked about helping them. Apparently several other listeners had also offered. Our country's problems are not the government's problems only. They're our problems as a society too.

Compassion involves empathy, understanding and concern for the suffering of others. It's an innate quality that all human beings possess, but it's not always at the forefront in our daily lives. It's a quality that can be difficult to cultivate and practise, especially in a world that is often characterised by cruelty, violence and indifference.

Compassion requires that we consistently demonstrate empathy and understanding towards those we disagree with. One of the most powerful examples of how Madiba showed compassion was after his visit to Yad Vashem, the World Holocaust Remembrance Center in Israel. When asked by the media for his impression of the museum, he said it was a terrible travesty and a blight on humanity that the world had allowed the Holocaust to happen. But then he added that the burden of the past was something the German people had to live with too.

He showed the ability to understand and share the feelings of others, taking into account all angles, as there can be more than one version of the truth. This involves putting yourself in someone else's shoes and seeing things from their perspective. This type of empathy is an important trait for effective leadership and self-development.

I was invited to Germany a few years ago at a time when people were demanding that all symbols and references to apartheid be removed from public life in South Africa. I agree that some symbols are too painful, such as the old South African flag. I have no problem with it being banned. I was, however, impressed to see in Berlin how the Germans had dealt with history in a brutal way. You can't walk two blocks without being reminded of Germany's role in the Second World War. Sometimes it's important to be reminded of something unconscionable so we never travel down that road again. It took the Germans more than 50 years to come to terms with their history, and it will take us a similar amount of time to deal with ours in a sensible way. When I see how passionately people defend symbolism, I'm reminded that my identity as a white, Afrikaans South African is not trapped in symbolism. There's a need for a more measured approach, and I believe we need to give people time to heal and build trust.

What we've learnt from history is that all people are fallible – our heroes included. When we choose to blindly rename things after people just because they're prominent names, we risk being disillusioned. Madiba personally cautioned against people naming halls, schools, roads and universities after him. It's something he simply didn't like.

He understood that for the country to avert civil war, it was necessary to show compassion in order to forgive and move forward. We hardly see this kind of empathy these days. He understood that everyone suffered under apartheid and that people's stories, from all walks of life, including those who had been his oppressors, were needed to develop an understanding of apartheid in the true sense. People need to be heard and understood, and it remains a great source of concern to me that, as a nation, we haven't dealt with the psychological impact of the past.

While attending to liberation-struggle veterans is on our country's agenda, we have, as a society, not paid enough attention to the large number of former soldiers from the apartheid regime who were sent to 'defend their country'. Young white men who were called up for compulsory military service at the age of eighteen are now in their fifties and sixties. Many live with post-traumatic stress disorder, as do countless MK veterans. The conscripts fought a war they knew little about because information was strictly controlled and, when you speak to them, it's clear that many of them bear resentment towards the apartheid regime. Their bottled-up anger – either at losing the fight or at having to surrender to the new dispensation – is an unexploded missile that can be detonated at any point. Of course, it's also true that many of them choose to remain in the past. But I often listen to stories of so-called 'war vets' in our country and worry about the energy we pass on to later generations because we haven't dealt with the past sufficiently.

Having empathy and compassion allows you to build strong relationships with people across the political spectrum, even those who you consider adversaries. Madiba realised that every person, irrespective of who or what they were, had something to contribute. In the age of smart phones, where cancel culture is rife, few people respect the fact that everyone has a unique perspective to share in life. To build coalitions that bring lasting change requires compassion, empathy and allowing the voices of adversaries to be heard. There is, however, a fine line between populism and sincere contributions. In our current politics, it's difficult to distinguish between the two.

More than one version
of the truth

We are humans that make mistakes.

– Nelson Mandela in conversation with Bill Clinton

It's human to be tempted to judge others when you haven't walked their path.

William Jefferson Clinton became the 42nd president of the United States of America a year before Nelson Mandela was sworn in as the first democratically elected president of South Africa. Presidents tend to forge relationships with their counterparts while in office. Most often, they're purely working relationships; occasionally, friendships evolve. This was the case with Madiba and President Bill Clinton.

They first met at a Democratic party convention in New York in 1992. During their meeting, Madiba said he was confident that Clinton would become an impactful, effective and efficient president of the US. A strong relationship with a president of the West – particularly the leader of the most powerful Western nation – was, of course, going to be beneficial to Madiba's presidency as it would have supported the ideals of the democracy he and his government wished to establish.

After that first meeting, the two men laid the foundation for a close friendship that would last until Madiba's passing in 2013. Apart from exchanging thoughts about business and politics, they often also spoke about life: raising children, dealing with emotions and disappointment, and battling the inner self while being overwhelmed by the business of being a world leader. They had a natural rapport built on mutual respect.

Not a lot has been written about Madiba's extramarital affairs during his first marriage to Evelyn Mase. He was young, handsome and popular among women. He's said to have been a charmer, but he was irresponsible. One is almost relieved to discover that even if he didn't have feet of clay, perhaps at least a toe or two were made of clay. For people who didn't know him, it makes 'Mandela, the icon' seem more human. On many occasions, he discouraged people from considering him a saint – unless they thought of a saint as a sinner who kept on trying. Perhaps, at first, our adoration and desperation for perfection prevented us from seeing those mistakes of his early years. With age, we tend to look back at our own mistakes and learn from them; I'm sure it was no different for Madiba.

Nevertheless, his reaction to the Bill Clinton and Monica Lewinsky saga provides insight, more than judgement, into dealing with infidelity. Shortly before President Clinton's 1998 state visit to South Africa, allegations emerged that he'd had an affair with an intern. I was 28 years old, opinionated and, quite frankly, rather judgemental. In a conversation with Madiba before the state visit, I gave my unsolicited opinion on the matter.

Those were the days before the internet and social media, but newspapers and TV stations carried daily snippets about the alleged affair. In January 1998, Clinton vehemently denied 'having sexual relations with that woman'. I was eager to get Madiba's take on the matter. Would it influence his relationship with President Clinton, and how would it affect his imminent state visit? Madiba didn't offer his opinion but said, 'To question a person's integrity without valid reason could well be a reflection of your own integrity,' and left it at that. It was important to him not to judge a person prematurely on any matter.

This has become almost impossible in the modern world, where group madness or collective hysteria, and herd mentality kick in because of social media. Very few of us can hold ourselves back from expressing judgement in any situation. And social media makes it so easy – in fact, it rewards us for our quick judgements. We have to be seen to be on one side or the other, for or against. We slaughter one another with judgements based on what we want to believe about a person or on what creates the best melodrama of the day. There was a time in my life when I, too, was active on social media, commenting on almost everything – until I experienced the damage it can do.

I have, on the odd occasion, reached out to people who have suffered the same fate because of something they did on social media. It's painful to watch, and often just expressing your concern goes a long way towards helping them survive the ordeal – like others did for me. It doesn't mean you're siding with a particular view. When expressing empathy and compassion, there's also no need to communicate your preferences. Instead, a kind word will help that person deal with the issue and give them the courage to work through their inner struggles and learn from the experience. I'll always remember those who reached out to me with empathy – not to reassure me but to help me reflect.

Madiba lived by a moral compass. To do so requires one to live with compassion and empathy.

After being impeached for perjury, Clinton admitted before a grand jury, in August 1998, to having had a sexual relationship with Monica Lewinsky. Just three months before, during his March visit, Clinton had received support and advice from his South African counterpart and friend. The advice did not directly address the affair; in true Madiba fashion, there were only hints of reference. The visit was aimed at strengthening bilateral relations between the US and South Africa and included an emotional visit to Robben Island where Madiba was incarcerated for eighteen of the 27 years of his imprisonment. I believe that the suffering Clinton felt at that moment in March – when he faced humiliation about his wrongdoing – was a poignant moment for the two men to connect on a much deeper level than just two presidents building diplomatic ties during a state visit. On that occasion, Madiba repeated the words he'd uttered during our discussion of the matter, and he didn't mention Monica's name once. And in that moment, he appealed to Clinton's integrity too.

Not long after President Clinton admitted to having had an affair with Monica Lewinsky, Madiba called his friend and said words to this effect:

> Bill, you made a mistake and you admitted to it. I have no doubt that you will finish your term, and I don't consider this to affect your ability to lead your country. We are humans that make mistakes. While dealing with this, you must now move forward and not allow your personal circumstance to overshadow the good that you have achieved and can bring to the world through your presidency.

It struck me that Madiba was always eager to show compassion to anyone who may be in distress. He appealed to their better nature and cast no aspersions on their mistakes – something that would have diminished his own humanity. Madiba addressed the charges by telling President Clinton that he'd made a mistake. It's simply not something you'd want Nelson Mandela to say to you; it would make it painful and real. That in itself must have been hard for Clinton to hear. I can imagine anyone feeling that the world could know about your mistake as long as Madiba did not – probably because he reflected what we so desperately wanted to be. We have incredibly fragile egos, and presidents are not spared either.

In another situation where he demonstrated great compassion, Madiba came to the rescue of one of the greatest sport stars of our time. In April 2000, we were in Ireland on business when news trickled in from the King Commission, established to investigate match-fixing in cricket involving the South African captain, Hansie Cronjé. With one voice, Madiba and I said, 'No, he's definitely not guilty.' We were being accommodated at the home of then CEO of Independent News & Media Sir Tony O'Reilly, and he was sceptical when he heard our response. So, I tried to establish whether he had insider information, since he was involved in the media. He laughed it off.

No, we knew Hansie, both Madiba and I maintained, supporting his denial of reports from India that he had been involved in wrongdoing. We'd left O'Reilly's residence to move on to our next destination when the call came from Prof Jakes Gerwel. 'Hansie admitted,' was all he said. We were devastated. We were travelling and unable to get a full report on the story because we had to rely on South African newspaper clippings being faxed to us the next day – yes, it was before the internet.

Personally, I felt devastated because Hansie was a close friend. How was this possible? As details emerged, it became clear that he had accepted money for information about an international match between India and South Africa. Although he didn't admit to match-fixing, he admitted to accepting the money to do it. Public outrage followed, and for days people wrote opinion pieces and analysed from head to toe the failed character of Hansie Cronjé. No one wanted to be associated with him, and his 'friends' all vanished, as well as sponsorships. His career came to an abrupt and humiliating end, and with it being loved by an entire nation. Today we would probably refer to it as cancel culture – on steroids.

When the media asked Madiba for comment, he said we should simply decline to comment. That was an extraordinary move. We always had 'something' to say. In the weeks that followed, there were articles, books, interviews, analyses . . . on repeat.

About six months later, the owners of Fancourt invited Madiba and Mrs Machel to relax at their upmarket golf estate and hotel near George in the Western Cape, where they were hosting a children's charity function. I mentioned to Madiba that Hansie and his wife,

Careless days during a holiday in Mauritius where Madiba enjoyed the sea as a holidaymaker for the first time. Mrs Machel and I would soak up the sun and swim regularly while he watched us from the porch of the villa. He then asked to join us, and as he was a little unstable on his feet already, we decided to put a plastic chair in the water from where he could enjoy the ocean as well.

During an interview to promote *Good Morning, Mr Mandela* internationally.

With Ahmed Kathrada, Zindzi Mandela and George Bizos at my book launch in 2014. They are sadly all deceased now.

Doing an interview about my first book with the inspirational motivational speaker Nicholas James Vujicic.

Karlien van Jaarsveld, Carien Loubser and Karen Zoid joined Bikers for Mandela Day and got their hands dirty by helping charitable organisations to improve the lives of the underprivileged.

Bikers for Mandela Day with two of the project's stalwart supporters, Pauli Massyn and Matthew Barnes. We had many happy moments and safe kilometres due to their involvement. They remind me of Madiba's saying: 'A good head and a good heart are always a formidable combination.'

DJ Fresh is a loyal supporter of Bikers for Mandela Day. If I didn't contact him fast enough, he would always reach out and offer his entire family's support.

Suddenly travelling alone without Madiba to promote *Good Morning, Mr Mandela*.
After twenty years of travelling, I finally got to know Manhattan, New York for
the first time. All the previous trips with Madiba were spent in hotels,
meeting rooms and event venues.

Rallying Springboks, sports and entertainment stars in support of Mandela Day. From left to right, top to bottom is Eben Etzebeth, Ryk Neethling, Siya Kolisi, Karen Zoid, Frans Malherbe, Siv Ngesi and Scarra Ntubeni.

In 2018, during Madiba's centenary celebrations, I was honoured to be the flag-bearer for the Springbok match in Port Elizabeth (now Gqeberha).

The horses that taught me about boundaries during horse therapy at the exclusive weekend hosted by Jeff Bezos in Sante Fe, USA.

Bertha, lived on the estate. Public outrage had died down, and Madiba announced that he wanted to see Hansie. Tea was arranged and Madiba instructed me to call the media so that he and Hansie could make a joint appearance after their engagement.

Hansie and Bertha received Madiba with open arms. It was plain to see that Hansie had been deeply damaged by events over the previous few months. Bertha, too, was a shadow of her former self. They were both emotional, and it was clear that they'd absorbed every punch thrown at them since the damning revelations. Madiba greeted them with his usual banter to try to ease the tension: 'Oh, Hansie, you have grown taller since I last saw you.' The irony of his comment wasn't lost on me. Although it was meant to disarm the couple, anyone could see that Hansie had shrunk, his shoulders drooping from the weight of his wrongdoing and the pain visible in the deeply etched lines on his face.

They sat down, and Madiba told them why he was in the picturesque town of George. He shared information irrelevant to their meeting to distract them from the anguish they were feeling. True to his character, he was appealing to their softer selves, hidden beneath the protective shell. There was no way to predict or anticipate what he would say next.

It was a well-known fact that Madiba was intolerant of dishonesty. He despised it. What would he say to them now that evidence was there in the form of Hansie's confession that he'd been dishonest and that he had let the country down? My heart bled for him. I was sitting in the background, trying to be invisible. Because we were friends, my presence was adding to Hansie's suffering, perhaps causing him to feel even more humiliated. One can only deal with so much disgrace, and having witnesses adds to the agony.

After an exchange of pleasantries and questions about the development of the estate, it was clear that the main purpose of the visit had to be addressed. There was silence. The room was electric with tension. I pretended to scribble on a piece of paper to avoid having to make eye contact with Hansie and Bertha – or with Madiba, for that matter.

I didn't know if he was going to reprimand or lash out at Hansie. He had disappointed the entire nation and the world of sport at large. People felt betrayed. There was anger and resentment; surely that was what Madiba felt too.

Although he was a guest in their house, he offered Hansie and Bertha more tea, just as we were expecting him to start the lecture. Instead, he lowered his voice and began speaking slowly, with intent in every word. 'Now, my boy,' he said. 'You made a big mistake.' Hansie nodded, tears welling up in his eyes.

Madiba didn't give the tears an opportunity to flow before he added, 'But you have admitted to the mistake, and you have apologised for it.' There was a barely audible sigh of relief, but Madiba quickly continued – Hansie was not off the hook yet. 'You now have to man up and face the consequences. But it doesn't mean that we love you less.' With so much compassion and understanding, he treated Hansie like a son.

I often refer to this incident when I talk about 'cancel culture' and how dispensable we make people in the age of smart phones. When someone makes a mistake, we cancel them and erase them from existence. We play judge and jury over people who err and prevent them from learning from the mistake because we discard them like used paper.

What Madiba did by verbalising what Hansie had done acknowledged that there was wrongdoing. It had to be said so that it was recorded, in no uncertain terms, that he did not approve of it.

He then acknowledged that Hansie had apologised, without judging the apology or questioning whether it was sincere. It brought to mind what he often said about integrity – in essence: who am I to decide whether an apology is sincere? What does it say about my integrity if I question the apology without being in a position to measure sincerity?

He told Hansie that there would be consequences, and the disgrace he felt was among them. And then came the lifeline – all that any person ever wants to hear: 'But it doesn't mean that we love you less.'

Madiba acknowledged Hansie's humanity, saying essentially that we knew he was human and would make mistakes, but we hoped he would learn from them. Seeing how this small gesture comforted Hansie as he dealt with the greatest crisis of his life made me realise that I should never underestimate the big importance of small acts.

It wasn't only public figures who drew Madiba's attention. In February 1999, a young black boy named Andrew Babeile stabbed a fellow pupil, a white boy named Christoff Erasmus, with a pair of scissors outside their school tuckshop in Vryburg in the North West province. It was branded a racial incident. Andrew was found guilty of attempted murder and sentenced to five years in prison, two of which were suspended for five years. After sentence was handed down in May 2000, just a month after the Hansie scandal broke, Madiba asked me to arrange for him to visit Andrew. He told the young man that no one can be reduced to only the sum of their worst mistakes or their best achievements, and that even though he now had to face the consequences of his actions by serving a prison sentence, he had the opportunity to better himself through education. He then arranged a bursary so that Andrew could use his time in prison to study, telling him that education was the only weapon to use to emerge from one's circumstances. Madiba's actions were based on his unshakeable belief that people could be better and do better, no matter their circumstances.

Having empathy with others doesn't mean that we blindly forgive or believe their narrative. It simply means we understand. Leave some margin for error. We are all so damn fallible, and Madiba understood that. By showing compassion to people in distress, Madiba understood and appreciated their complexity as human beings.

Revenge becomes
a self-inflicted wound

*If you want to make peace with your enemy, you have to
work with your enemy. Then he becomes your partner.*

– Nelson Mandela

I can't help wishing that I'd had the opportunity to discuss my mistakes with Madiba. I wonder what his response may have been to my tweets. One of the things that carried me through the experience was knowing that he would have reprimanded me in no uncertain terms, but then reminded me that no one was without mistakes and assured me of his love. It was in this moment that I missed him the most.

In his book *So You've Been Publicly Shamed*, British journalist and author Jon Ronson writes that we lose our individuality through mob justice when we're judging others. We create a society in which people are too afraid to make mistakes because they fear being cancelled. How do you learn if not from mistakes? We therefore become more reserved in being and expressing ourselves, and we inhibit our emotions, which prevents us from learning or expanding our views. People's desperation for popularity drives them to assume the head boy or head girl role, policing everyone else and deciding who's right or wrong by shaming them whenever there's a misstep. Until it happens to them.

It always amazes me how people can judge someone's character based on one action when they know absolutely nothing about the person. When you don't know their character and sense of humour, the type of language they use and, most importantly, their *intent*, how do you judge a stranger?

Good leaders allow people to make mistakes, recognising that it's part of human nature. They know that fear and shame are not helpful when creating policies and strategies; they result in people being too afraid to voice their opinions because they don't know which issues they may or may not be 'right' about. It's become the privilege of publicly anonymous people to make and learn from mistakes; any remotely recognisable person doesn't have that luxury anymore because they're likely to be crucified and discarded. It's referred to as the David vs Goliath syndrome. And within that scenario, individuals try to gain popularity by being a smart arse – the first to express the punchline that brings someone down – and gaining likes and retweets that will elevate their status. In their own world, that is.

Over the years, I've considered with curiosity a few cases similar to that of Hansie Cronjé. Part of the moral decay in society is that we're selective in our judgement of people. To what standard do we, personally, hold individuals? If it's a friend transgressing, our judgement might be totally different from when it's a stranger or a common enemy.

When well-known economist and commentator Thabi Leoka was found to have lied about a PhD qualification from the London School of Economics, she was summarily cancelled on social media. She's not a fan of mine, but as I witnessed her demise, I felt deeply sorry for her. No one should have to live through a cruel public shaming on social media. In many instances, it's become a cheap tool to settle scores instead of being used to express disapproval of wrongdoing.

Interestingly, some of those who usually occupied front-row seats in the cancel-culture show were nowhere to be seen because Leoka was a friend. In fact, they didn't go onto social media for days until the storm had passed. Don't get me wrong: I'm absolutely against public shaming. My point here, though, is that people who make cancel culture their business are often selective in applying it. Perhaps they hope that, while firing salvos of disdain at selected targets, they will successfully zigzag or be elusive enough to dodge the word bullets that could, at any time, be fired back at them.

In her book *When Love Kills: The Tragic Tale of AKA and Anele*, South African journalist and author Melinda Ferguson refers to how the social media machine accused rapper and record producer AKA (Kiernan Forbes) 'of all sorts of damning things' after the death of his fiancée, Anele Tembe. But two years later, after AKA was murdered, 'he emerged saviour-like, risen from the tomb of a modern-day Golgotha, to become a national hero'.

How selective our outrage has become, I thought after reading this. Surely we can't deal with misogyny and sexism adequately if we're going to be selective about what we condone in society.

I agree wholeheartedly with Ferguson's take on cancel culture – that 'sometimes it feels expedient and counterproductive to erase people when difficult conversations are needed instead'. She continues: 'I believe that the cancer of silence that shrouds abuse or problematic behaviour is perpetuated when we erase the perpetrator. It's vital that we maintain an open dialogue and revisit these stories so that we don't simply bury atrocities and move on. That's too easy.'

My friends and family were angry at those who were honest with me about my Twitter faux pas. However, once I'd regained my footing after the initial shock, I appreciated their honesty – that they were fair and kept their professional integrity intact. If they hadn't, I would now be questioning their judgement over matters in which I can't discern right from wrong because I don't have all the facts.

Surely the way to correct society is not to bury thorny issues by simply shutting someone down – effectively 'cancelling' their participation in the public debate. Let's call, instead, on a mature and pragmatic understanding of our common frailty so that, like Madiba, we treat the *person* with empathy and compassion without condoning their misdeeds. Isn't that how we transform society?

Whenever a Michael Jackson song is played on the radio, I'm on my feet, singing and dancing to his music. It's only by the second verse that I find myself thinking about what I'm doing. The allegations of child molestation have irreparably damaged the King of Pop's legacy, but I wonder: is it not possible to separate the human being and his transgressions from the musical genius? Do we discard his life's work because he spectacularly failed to be an exemplary, morally flawless human being?

In no way should we condone actions of violence or abuse by anyone, famous or not, especially against women and children, but I often think of Madiba and invoke his measured approach towards matters. Very good people can be tempted to do very bad things.

In 2016, Microsoft unveiled an artificial intelligence chatbot called Tay. She was designed to learn to communicate through Twitter by mimicking what she found on the internet. Within sixteen hours, Tay's life was abruptly terminated because she'd turned into a misogynist and racist parrot that even referred to feminism as a cult and a cancer. The flaming garbage pile that went in was the same flaming garbage pile that came out. Tay assimilated the internet's worst tendencies. But these tendencies weren't created by the internet; people behind their keyboards were responsible – real humans who always had a choice to decide whether to press 'send'.

Instead of raining down vengeance on a person who's made a mistake, how about we say: 'You've made a mistake. You've admitted and apologised for it, and for that we applaud you. You'll now have to face the consequences of your actions, but know that we'll be here when you reach the other side.' Because that is exactly what Madiba would have done.

When last did you see someone showing empathy and compassion rather than unmitigated outrage and cruelty? Are we all living up to Madiba's standards?

Madiba understood his power, but more importantly he understood when not to use it. He had the power to exercise revenge against his former enemies, yet he understood that revenge becomes a self-inflicted wound.

It must be possible to admit that someone has grossly failed yet still appreciate their achievements. In my personal life, I've struggled with this too. I so desperately want to be like Madiba, but I struggle to forgive people who have hurt or damaged me or others. The trauma lives with me every day and, although I work hard at not repeating the same mistakes, I struggle to engage with hypocrites or people who are cruel. I can't bring myself to socialise with those who have taken part in bringing someone down and then pretended that their actions were innocent. But I hold no grudges. I've learnt to move on and not allow things to fester. People like you as long as you do what they do and expect of you, including speaking badly of others. Once you set your boundaries, they start disliking you. But you learn to understand how important boundaries are for your own wellbeing.

We're on a continuous path of self-discovery, which also involves learning that you can't hold people to different standards from what you expect of yourself. As an extension of this, I've become better at accepting that it's not my duty to teach people lessons by confronting every situation I come across. I'm a firm believer that we all travel our own journey, and the mistakes I've made taught me valuable lessons. Now I shouldn't deny another person the opportunity to learn through their mistakes.

In many instances, when Madiba had reached the end of his relationship with someone, he would simply withdraw without announcement or fanfare. He hardly ever spoke badly of anyone, but his actions, or simply his failure to maintain certain friendships or relationships, were enough to read his position on a particular person.

About a year into his presidency, he invited state prosecutor Percy Yutar to lunch. Yutar was the man who'd been at the helm of the state's case against the accused in the Rivonia Trial in 1964, which led to Madiba and his co-accused being sentenced to life imprisonment.

During the last years of Madiba's incarceration, Yutar asked to see him, and the request was put to him by the minister of justice at the time, Kobie Coetsee. Madiba agreed, but the visit never came about. By the time the two men met for lunch in November 1995, they were both advanced in years. Madiba wanted to show Yutar that he held no resentment. In the press conference after the lunch, Yutar extended his gratitude to Madiba and referred to him as 'saintly'. In turn, Madiba said that compared to the architect of apartheid, Hendrik Verwoerd, Yutar's role had been a small one. For Madiba, it was enough that Yutar had been extended an opportunity to redeem himself; in my view, an apology from Yutar would have been appropriate.

In his book *Winnie and Nelson: Portrait of a Marriage*, Jonny Steinberg argues that actions such as meeting and shaking hands with his former enemies may have involved some deliberate vindictiveness on Madiba's part. That may be his view, but this was not my experience at all. Madiba knew that by forgiving those who'd wronged him or those who'd inflicted pain on him, he also afforded them the chance to forgive themselves and break free from the torture they might be putting themselves through. He often said that holding on to resentment was like drinking poison while hoping your enemy would die.

Living with your own actions can be as painful as the deed itself.

Providing the opportunity for someone like Yutar to face his demons was the most liberating gift Madiba could give. He did it so that the person could live in peace with themselves and neither party would be drinking their own 'poison' – resentment.

It was only years later that I really understood that redemption was often not accompanied by the words we wanted to hear. Sometimes a simple act of kindness provides that opportunity too. Redemption doesn't look and sound the way we expect it to, and the following experience taught me exactly that. In 2016, South Africa's top detective, Piet Byleveld, was diagnosed with stage-four lung cancer. Madiba had met Piet after his brilliant detective work had led to the arrest and prosecution of some of the most notorious murderers in our history. He was known as the most successful serial-killer hunter and super-sleuth in South Africa. When he met Madiba at our offices in Houghton, Johannesburg, his authenticity impressed me. I had his mobile phone number and, when the report of his diagnosis reached the media, I sent him a message of encouragement, saying this would be his biggest case in life and that he simply had to crack it too. I wished him a speedy and complete recovery, and we agreed to stay in touch.

In mid-May 2017, I was on a game farm with patchy reception when I received a missed-call notification from Piet. When I returned the call, his wife, Elize, answered the phone. It was actually she who had called to let me know that Piet was in hospital and that the prognosis wasn't good. I promised to visit when I got back to Johannesburg a few days later. When I arrived at the hospital, a group of people were gathered outside, taking a break in the autumn sunshine, but as I'd never met Elize, I didn't realise she was among them. The nurses showed me to Piet's room. He was already in a coma and breathing heavily. The ward was cold, the curtains half-drawn; Piet's brother, Willie, and one of his friends sat slouched in visitors' chairs between the bed and the window. After introducing myself, I turned my attention to Piet: he looked peaceful and in a deep sleep. He'd never been a large man, but now he looked shrunken. I noticed there were no machines attached to him and realised there was nothing more the doctors could do for him. His death was imminent.

Willie told me Elize was outside taking a break but that I was welcome to speak to Piet and wait for her to return. I leant in close to Piet's ear and told him quietly that he was brave, that I wished him well and that he should never forget how loved and appreciated he was by all South Africans.

It's often the caregivers and family of people in such situations who need the extra care and an embrace, so I started to make conversation with Willie. He then told me about a strange occurrence three nights before. At the time, Piet was in a ward with three other people, and the man in the bed next to him was also gravely ill with a similar condition. Like Piet, the man was struggling to breathe; nonetheless, Piet had helped him whenever he could to get to the bathroom or when he needed water. The next day, Piet had begun to slip in and out of deep sleep, and when he was awake, he struggled to get to the bathroom. His neighbour, who was then a little stronger, helped Piet to the toilet during the night before the nursing staff could be called for help. It was a hellish night for them both, as they were struggling to breathe and needed oxygen. During visiting time, a member of the man's family came to Piet's bed to tell him that the man was an ex-convict, someone that Piet had sent to prison through his police work many years before. On the same day, Piet was sedated as his condition had deteriorated, and he was transferred to the single-bed ward.

Tears welled up in my eyes as I realised that the ex-convict had to help Piet to the toilet that night because *he* needed that opportunity, through a simple act of kindness, for redemption. As Piet's brother was telling the story, Elize entered. Piet was completely unresponsive but, while holding his hand and stroking his chest, Elize added details to the story. As she finished, I said, 'Elize, that's the most beautiful story I've ever heard, and it's what I really think is the purpose of life – for us to allow people to redeem themselves, to create those opportunities so that others can free themselves.' I said it seemed that this ex-convict had to pay his dues by helping Piet that night. 'He actually also forgave Piet, even though Piet did what he was expected to do in his job – convict criminals – but the part in it for us is that we're dealing with human beings who need redemption even when in the wrong.' There was no way the man could *not* have known that the person he was helping was Piet Byleveld. I was deeply touched by the story and, while everyone was looking at me as I spoke, I glanced at Piet and realised he'd stopped breathing. I calmly said, 'Elize, Piet has stopped breathing,' and quietly left the room before running to the nurses' station to call for help. There was nothing they could do. He was gone.

Although it was one of the saddest things to witness, it was also a privilege to see someone crossing from this life with such peace in that moment. I'm a firm believer that when you're granted the opportunity of being in the presence of someone who's dying, all you have to do is let them know that they're loved and appreciated. At the end of the day, that's all we crave as human beings and the only thing of substance we can take with us to the grave.

In that moment, I understood why Madiba believed that no one was beyond redemption. We all make mistakes, and it's not the mistake that defines you but how you learn from it.

'Very well, yes, I see'

No one is incapable of forgiving, and no one is unforgivable.

– Desmond Tutu, *The Book of Joy*

To inspire compassion takes effort, and the two people who demonstrated that best were Nelson Mandela and Archbishop Desmond Tutu. After Madiba's death, I stayed in touch with the Arch, as he was fondly known, and his wife, whom I call Aunt Leah. I often visited them when I was in Cape Town and was acutely aware of the Arch's deteriorating health as age crept in.

I was heartbroken that people felt I'd betrayed them through my tweets in 2015. Many didn't mention it, but my own insecurities made me reach out to people I felt I could have hurt or disappointed. One such person was Archbishop Tutu. I joked with him that God would not forgive me if he didn't forgive me, and the Arch responded with his characteristic high-pitched laugh.

We had tea and he prayed for me, holding hands with me and Aunt Leah. He prayed for those who harboured anger and hatred and, on conclusion of his prayer, I commented that I didn't think some people would ever forgive me. He got a little angry and said, 'South Africans are the most forgiving people in the world!' It made me think. We are.

For the sake of political point-scoring, opportunists will draw blood from a stone to prove the opposite, but in truth most South Africans have contributed to the peaceful transition in our country. The Arch had first-hand experience of people testifying at the Truth and Reconciliation Commission (TRC), which he'd chaired. The aim of the commission was to seek forgiveness from both sides and, in many instances, to allow closure for those who never had a body to bury or hadn't known how a loved one had died. In many instances, it took the admittedly enormous step for people to say 'I forgive' to free not only the perpetrator from guilt, but also the victim from crippling resentment.

In *The Book of Joy* by the Dalai Lama and Archbishop Desmond Tutu, the Arch says: 'We cannot say of anyone at all that they are totally unable to forgive. I think that all of us have the latent potential, as His Holiness is pointing out, to be sorry for these others who are disfiguring their humanity in this way. Indeed, no one is incapable of forgiving, and no one is unforgivable.'

I, too, had to forgive those who'd poured so much hate over me, and I found it within myself to do so. Forgiveness doesn't mean you have to have a relationship with the person who has harmed you. But it does open the way for creating inner peace for both parties. If we believe that Madiba did not forgive people such as Percy Yutar but rather that he met his former enemies for vindictive reasons, we forget the importance of Madiba also requiring inner peace and needing to let go of the other's throat so he could continue life without holding grudges.

When Yutar returned to Madiba a second time, asking him for help with selling the Rivonia Trial documents – which he must have kept from his days in government – Madiba simply did not respond to the request. Yutar knew, from Madiba's silence, that he'd gone too far. Forgiving someone does not mean you should allow the person to take advantage of your goodwill or your grace. Naturally, Madiba was also angered by Yutar's audacious approach – after all, he was seeking to profit from Madiba's suffering. But he didn't express that in so many words. Those of us who were close to Madiba knew that his refusal to act on a request from someone spoke a thousand times more loudly than any verbal explanation could.

Whenever I visited the Arch and Aunt Leah after Madiba's passing, they welcomed me with open arms. I think I saw more of them after Madiba died than during the entire time I'd worked for him. Their home in Milnerton became a welcome sanctuary from the noise of the outside world. I was told a month before the Arch's death in 2021 that he'd stopped eating. Knowing very well that it may be the last time I would see him, I paid him a visit; it was deeply upsetting to see him bedridden. He was among the last great spirits of a generation of selfless and dedicated men and women who helped to liberate our country.

Despite his ill health, he sat upright in his bed when I arrived. I said, 'Arch, hello, it's the ousie coming to see you.' Ousie is an Afrikaans word used during apartheid to describe black helpers in households. The Arch had a well-known, impish sense of humour and his pet name for me was in no way meant to demean but rather to jokingly refer to 'the help' and to make light of what is now considered an offensive word. I loved it.

He smiled and took my hand. 'God bless you, Ousie, God bless you.' I told him how much I loved him, how much he meant to me and the world, and that he should never forget how well loved and appreciated he was.

He passed away the day after Christmas.

I had the enormous honour of saying goodbye to our beloved Arch in a speech I delivered at a memorial service held at the Desmond & Leah Tutu Legacy Foundation. I said that he was the first person I'd met in the Presidency in 1994, and that this 'small-figured man wearing a cassock' was the complete opposite of how he'd been depicted in the apartheid media – as an outspoken troublemaker who hated whites. 'Archbishop Desmond Tutu was friendly, warm and made you feel completely comfortable in his presence, as if you had arrived home after a long absence.' In his presence, you never felt you had to behave in a particular way because he was a cleric. My experience was that he understood his calling not to mean that he should exercise superiority or act as the judge and jury over another man's life, 'but rather to listen, understand and lead the way to a path of greater good for the self and others. He taught us that no one was beyond redemption by seeking healing, even for his opponents'.

I said I'd quickly picked up on the Arch's brilliant sense of humour:

> I laugh when I think of the time the Arch commented on Madiba wearing his signature shirts when he ought to have worn a suit, and Madiba hit back by saying that he didn't take fashion instructions from a man wearing a dress. Today such comments would be frowned upon, but it was part of the innocent banter between the two wise old owls.
>
> Madiba said that there were two types of leaders: those who were consistent and those who were inconsistent. His [The Arch's] consistent pursuit of fairness, forgiveness, equality, peace and harmony took centre stage every day of his life. He did not shy away from criticising anyone out of fear of being shamed or being unpopular. Without fail, he did what was expected of us as human beings, as the best version of ourselves.

I went on to speak about how, for many years, the Arch had absorbed, digested and lived with the pain of victims and their families revealed during the TRC hearings. 'The process was not flawless, as we know, but it created an opportunity for us to deal with our past and for ordinary folks to give each other permission to heal. To honour Archbishop Tutu's legacy, it falls upon us as a generation to do exactly that.'

More than 60 countries were due to go to the polls in 2024. Will voters across the globe be influenced by populism, or will the legacies of people like Madiba and the Arch persuade them to choose leaders with similar qualities? Will we choose a world in which black and white, Muslim and Jew, refugee and citizen can live side by side, or will hatred and discord continue to flourish? In creating a leadership model, we have the perfect examples in Madiba and the Arch. Our memories of them are still fresh, and their acts of compassion and forgiveness remain relevant not just for leaders but for everyone, every day.

Madiba was generous with his compassion and often extended it to individuals beyond our borders. But compassion didn't make him a soft-touch leader: under certain circumstances, he showed that he couldn't abide others having the opportunity to show compassion but wilfully rejecting it – especially when they were in a position of power and leadership. In 1995, Nigerian military head of state Sani Abacha called for the execution of nine leaders of the Movement for the Survival of the Ogoni People, reportedly on trumped-up murder charges. In reality, their 'transgression' was to criticise the Nigerian military government for refusing to sanction international oil companies that had caused environmental damage in the Niger Delta region, threatening the livelihood of Ogoniland residents. Ken Saro-Wiwa and eight others were sentenced to death. During a visit to the country Madiba pleaded with various politicians in Nigeria not to execute the Ogoni Nine, as they were known, but he was unable to move Abacha. In a follow-up visit by then Deputy President Thabo Mbeki, during which he reiterated the request, Abacha undertook to use his presidential prerogative to show leniency if the Ogoni Nine were found guilty and sentenced to death. Despite Abacha's undertaking, Saro-Wiwa and his co-accused were executed. It angered Madiba, and he called for oil sanctions against the military regime.

In contrast to the bold political and leadership statement this conveyed, Madiba often showed his sincere concern and compassion for individuals who were out of the limelight. One example is particularly close to my heart because it involved my father. Late one night, we flew from Pretoria to Cape Town on the presidential plane and arrived about an hour later than expected. The Ysterplaat Air Force Base where the presidential plane landed was already closed. Although the station

113

commander was there to receive us, the building used as a lounge for VIPs was dark. When the plane touched down, it was already 10 pm. Madiba asked, as he usually did, if I had transport to take me home. I sometimes wondered whether, if I'd said no, he'd have offered to take me home with his convoy. I'm sure that would have been eventful!

I told him that I'd asked my father to collect me. My parents were living in Cape Town at the time and were eager for me to spend every spare moment I had with them. I didn't see them often because, as mentioned, I would spend almost every Christmas, New Year and holiday with Madiba and Mrs Machel.

Madiba asked if my father knew the plane was late, and I explained that I hadn't been able to let him know from Pretoria before take-off. (Those were the days before everyone had a mobile phone.) He was perturbed because a delay on his side at home in Johannesburg had caused us to be late.

The plane came to a standstill after taxiing to the arrivals terminal. It was raining, and the cold Cape winter's night seemed particularly stormy and dark. When I said my goodbyes to Madiba, he took my arm and asked about my father. I pointed towards his car, indicating that my dad was waiting for me in his vehicle. 'No, no, no,' said Madiba. 'Please tell him to come here.' I was tired and cold and knew that the bodyguards and commanding officer of the air force base, as well as the pilots, were all eager to get back to their families and their warm homes as soon as possible.

Despite feeling slightly irritated because I was fully aware that we'd be delaying all the other personnel not included in this little rendezvous, I called my dad closer as I dropped my suitcase in the boot of his car. Madiba greeted my dad warmly and asked the commander whether he could open the VIP lounge because he wanted to see my dad inside. The commander rushed to fetch the keys to the building. Once inside, he switched on the lights while Madiba invited my dad to sit down. Very much aware of the people outside in their cars, desperate to go home, I thought: what now?

Madiba looked at the commander and said, 'Do you think there's a possibility for us to have a cup of coffee?' Who could say no to the president? I rushed to the kitchen with the commander to prepare the coffee and tray while trying to apologise for the delay. But the commander was friendly and welcomed every opportunity to interact with Madiba. We hadn't taken coffee orders before going to the kitchen, but I decided my father was having coffee whether he wanted it or not. Returning to the conversation with the coffee – in small cups, as Madiba preferred, which meant instant coffee in an espresso-sized cup – I was eager to hear what the hoo-ha was about, the reason for this ceremonial pause. What had my father done that Madiba had summoned him? Or, more seriously, what had I done? I was somewhat nervous, hoping that I hadn't done anything wrong that Madiba now wanted to discuss with my father. I felt like a schoolgirl whose teacher was about to discuss her progress on parents' evening.

But the conversation was going nowhere. They were talking about whatever was going on in the country at the time, until I said, 'Khulu, I think the people outside are eager to get home. Perhaps we should call it a night.' He then said he was just apologising to my father for being late and for causing an inconvenience.

I was touched, and of course my father greatly appreciated the gesture. I felt deeply sorry for the commander too, but the more I apologised, the more he made light of it. I thought about the security guards who were also delayed by our late arrival and wondered if Madiba had also apologised to them.

This was just another example of Madiba's thoughtfulness and being consistently mindful of others. By being considerate, showing compassion and listening with the intention of understanding another person's point of view, we build meaningful relationships.

Sadly, my experience in recent times is very different. We listen to respond, not to comprehend, so we don't truly hear each other. Make any statement on social media and you'll receive a vast variety of responses that will demonstrate that people either read what you *didn't* say or made assumptions about what you *did* say. It's a recipe for disaster.

I have a friend who makes a point of asking her children to repeat her instructions or reflect back to her what they've heard. It's fascinating to observe how we tend to interpret or misinterpret things. My friend is trying to teach her children not to assume anything, which is admirable and probably requires you to have the patience and wit that she has.

Novelist Ernest Hemingway famously said, 'When people talk, listen completely. Don't be thinking about what you're going to say. Most people never listen. Nor do they observe.'

Interestingly, Madiba's first childhood memory was about learning the art of listening. As a young boy, he would be allowed to attend meetings of the elders. The sole purpose of the leader of the meeting was to listen and then summarise all the input at the end of the meeting.

That had an unquestionable influence on Madiba's own ability to listen. He listened to world leaders, elders and children. In fact, he sought out divergent voices because he believed that the most effective way of making decisions was to consider all points of view.

One of my favourite memories of Madiba is how he would lean into a conversation with his hands folded or with one hand on his chin, listening attentively. At the end of your submission, there would be a long pause. Then he would simply say, 'Very well, yes, I see.' And that meant that he *did* see you, and he had heard your views. But it did not necessarily mean he agreed with you. In that moment, he'd listened and fully observed.

Madiba inspired loyalty in people because he showed empathy, compassion and mindfulness. He created an inclusive environment based on understanding and respect. These actions were not limited to me only. He always enquired about the wellbeing of everyone around him. At any point, he was aware of his staff's circumstances and the concerns people felt. Taking that into consideration allowed him to create a positive and supportive working environment that encouraged growth and development.

He always knew exactly the progress of his household staff's children. He helped many of them through school – something he took on in addition to his own family responsibilities. Education was critical to him, and he was willing to support the children of those who worked for him to impress upon them just how important it was.

Looking at life from all angles

The single story creates stereotypes, and the problem with stereotypes is not that they are untrue, but that they are incomplete. They make one story become the only story.

– Chimamanda Ngozi Adichie, TED talk, 'The Danger of a Single Story'

I, like countless others, was deeply distressed by the death of the African-American George Floyd in 2020, and by the brutal events that led to it. He was accosted by police on suspicion of having used a counterfeit $20 bill at a convenience store. A video of his arrest – showing Minneapolis police officer Derek Chauvin kneeling on his neck and back while he was handcuffed, face down, for over nine minutes – went viral internationally and ignited a wave of protests against racism, as well as the widespread use of the Black Lives Matter hashtag. The cruelty on display by Chauvin and three other police officers, despite Floyd calling for help and telling them he couldn't breathe, was heartbreaking. It sparked a worldwide debate about police brutality, as well as racism in general. For more than 300 years, only white lives mattered. During slavery, colonialism and apartheid, black lives didn't matter as much as white lives, and no one can deny that. The education system, religion and the media supported the belief that white people were brought up with: that they were superior. Advertising campaigns reinforced this belief: the 'perfect family' was a white heterosexual couple with two children. Black people were excluded from numerous rights and opportunities, including access to quality education and social services such as healthcare, political rights and land ownership, and subjected to restrictive employment practices. All of this gave white people an advantage in life, and when people point to white privilege, it partly refers to advances like these that we received purely based on the colour of our skin.

The protests that followed the death of George Floyd reinvigorated the Black Lives Matter movement, which was started in 2013 to highlight racial injustice. At its core, the #BlackLivesMatter campaign is a cry from people who want to be acknowledged. It draws attention not just to racial injustice but also to systemic racism and police brutality.

While Floyd came to represent all black people who'd been victimised by racism, the white cop signified the deep-rooted injustices still present in societal institutions such as law and education – systemic racism. In reality, there are criminals everywhere. Yes, black and white. In every society, you'll find the worst and best of humankind.

When people say black lives matter, they don't mean to say no other lives matter. Why are people hearing or implying that? They don't mean that farmers' lives do not matter. They don't mean that vulnerable women's and children's lives do not matter, or that they matter less. They don't mean that a hardened criminal's life matters more. It is a call to be listened to and to be understood, without dismissing another person's feelings, experiences and thoughts.

They mean to say that after so many years of injustice, they want to be recognised and treated as equals. In this instance, the focus is a plea for acknowledgement that no one is superior to anyone else. Also, even if we say we're equal, we must acknowledge the impact of colonialism, systemic racism and unconscious biases, and that economic and social inequalities disproportionately affect black communities. To simply say that we're all equal does not make us all equal and does not undo many years of inequality. It also does not undo the years of colonialism, slavery and inherent white privilege – the legacy that can't be denied and that is still very much present. As much as we need to address unconscious bias, we also need to address unconscious privilege.

No person's identity can be credited or discredited because of the behaviour of another man or woman. Generalisation is dangerous and grossly unfair. If you generalise, you say that simply because many movies have been made about Mexican drug lords, all Mexicans are drug traffickers. Or you've read 100 articles about black murderers, therefore all black people are murderers (or you've read 100 stories about white people being racist, so all white people are racist). Because the US is known to enter war, all Americans are war lords. Because movies are made about Italian Mafia bosses, all Italians work for Mafia syndicates. We simply cannot reduce people's behaviour to generalisations, movie plots or stereotypical storylines. It is also important to understand that these generalisations, or dominant societal narratives, have been constructed to divide and are steeped in various forms of inequality based on race, gender, class and sexuality.

Madiba, too, had different experiences with people of all races but chose not to see everyone through the same lens. His first close interaction with a white family was in 1934 when he met Reverend Cecil Harris, the head of Clarkebury Methodist School, where the young Madiba was sent to board. He later wrote that he admired Rev Harris and how he ran the school 'with an iron hand and an abiding sense of fairness'.

At the school, he encountered many students from different cultures but grew close to Rev Harris's family, often receiving special treatment due to a direct request from the regent, Madiba's custodian after the passing of his father.

A few years later, the young Nelson Mandela and the regent's son, his cousin, Justice Dalindyebo, ran away from arranged marriages. While they were trying to escape the regent's plans for them, a white woman in Queenstown in the Eastern Cape gave them a lift to Johannesburg. This was in the 1940s, when suspicion between white and black flourished.

Yet the woman decided to give the two young men a chance. By showing them compassion, she forever changed the course of Nelson Mandela's life. In *Winnie and Nelson: Portrait of a Marriage*, Steinberg describes how Madiba and Justice had to change seats because the woman mistrusted Justice, who was the more jubilant and rowdier of the two boys. One must remind oneself that during those years it was highly unusual for a white woman to have two black men in her car. Propaganda and indoctrination by the white system fomented fear and distrust of blacks, particularly emphasising the danger that black men allegedly posed to white women.

In the same book, Steinberg describes a scene during Madiba's days as an articled clerk at the Johannesburg law firm Witkin, Sidelsky & Eidelman. When he was dictating notes to a white secretary and white clients entered the office for appointments with the lawyers, the secretary would pretend that Madiba was a messenger, hand him a few coins and send him to the shop to buy shampoo for her. It must have been a very humiliating experience. The same woman suggested that the young clerk use a particular cup for his coffee at the office. He was not meant to use the same cups as the white employees.

Madiba's experiences involving people of different races prevented him from buying into the dogma that any one person of a particular race will always mirror the behaviour of either the worst or best of that racial group.

We dare not give up on one another. We should never stop trying. There's always the possibility that things will get better – and they will, but it requires commitment, courage and control. Yes, control over the self and constantly encouraging ourselves to grow, understand and be aware that we have unconscious biases about others and ourselves.

Black Lives Matter is not asking for a response other than for people to acknowledge the fact that black lives do, indeed, matter. Have white people really walked in the shoes of a black person to the extent that they can claim to understand, and then have the right to respond with an 'all lives matter' chant? I don't believe so.

Nelson Mandela was imprisoned for 27 years by the apartheid state – a state built on segregation and discrimination. Yet it did not make him hate white people. He despised the system that was carefully created to exclude most South African citizens from the vote, the economy and so much else. There are no ifs and buts. Just acknowledging that is the starting point of many solutions around us. But our fragile egos and fear of retribution prevent us from opening the door to healing ourselves and others.

We overcame apartheid because the people of our country decided to work together rather than destroy one another and, in doing so, our entire country.

Sometimes it requires us just to listen and have compassion. The fact that George Floyd was a second offender or had allegedly taken drugs on that fateful day is not relevant to the way he was treated. His past should be of no consequence to anyone. It amazes me how some people want us to consider Floyd's past transgressions, but when their own transgressions are highlighted they are quick to clap back and tell people to 'move on'. I always put myself in the shoes of someone like that. How would I have felt if it was me, or if it was my brother and the roles were reversed? Do I show sufficient compassion in circumstances like that?

But then, the same goes for the police officers. What they did was inhumane, brutal and unacceptable and deserves condemnation by the law. They were charged, found guilty and sent to prison. They now live with the consequences every single minute they spend in their prison cells. The nine minutes in which they made the worst mistake of their lives will haunt them until the day they die. The punishment of living with the sin eating at you every day for the rest of your life is often greater than the sin itself. Such behaviour can never be condoned and should serve as a historic reminder of how systemic inequality works.

However, is it possible to also have compassion with them without condoning their behaviour? Indeed, in a moment of extreme anger or when we are flustered, we don't think clearly or consider all the possible outcomes of a situation. We simply don't. That can be a life-changing mistake. The justice system provides for restorative justice, but our duty as human beings, as Madiba said, is to look at things from all angles and show compassion – even in the most challenging situations. If he was able to have compassion even for his jailers, having focused his anger on the system and not those who interpreted the laws made by the system, then we can approach difficult situations like that too.

I was reminded of this when a man in a small town north of Pretoria raped and assaulted his girlfriend and left her for dead. Johan Kotze became known as the Modimolle Monster after what he had done to his girlfriend. But Archbishop Tutu cautioned the public, reminding us that the man was not a monster but a human being created by God – one who had made terrible mistakes.

If such cruel harm was done to me, I don't know whether I'd be able to forgive, but writing this and thinking about these instances help me remind myself to view things from all angles, as Madiba did.

During his address to the World Conference against Racism, Racial Discrimination, Xenophobia and Related Intolerance in Durban in September 2001, Madiba referred to his inaugural address as president of a newly democratic and non-racial South Africa, in which he said that out of the experience of an extraordinary human disaster that had lasted too long had to be born a society of which all humanity would be proud. That had been the challenge not just for South Africa but also the whole world. He continued:

Racism is often described as a disease. And that is a problem for all of us. Racism is an ailment of the mind and soul. It kills many more than any contagion; it dehumanises anyone it touches. The tragedy is that a cure is within our reach, yet we have not seized it. The defeat of apartheid was a victory, but apartheid was only a symptom of the disease. To conquer racism, we must administer a treatment that is comprehensive and holistic.

The job of the conference delegates was to look for a global response to a problem afflicting all of our countries. 'History has made us what we are. But we do not have to be bound by history – we can also decide to make our own destinies,' he said, adding that he hoped the conference would be remembered as one where people from around the world undertook 'to cherish and value diversity, to coexist in a spirit of mutual respect, to understand that to deny the humanity of the other is to deny oneself'.

And then, his impassioned call: 'Let this be a time for healing old wounds. Let this be a time to reach out to each other across the real or imaginary divides. Let this be a time to build a true spirit of solidarity in support of human dignity.'

Madiba set the tone for dealing with racism: while we cannot be disentangled from our past, we have to employ care in dealing with issues that stem from centuries of hatred and discord, in order to find a way forward.

When a South African woman journalist was captured on camera requiring black but not white politicians to put on their face masks before being interviewed during the Covid-19 pandemic, she was immediately condemned and sent to Twitter hell. Apart from suffering emotional trauma, she was branded professionally too. Social media users sometimes behave like a pack of wild dogs running after an injured animal until they're distracted by the next victim along the way. Unfortunately, no lessons are ever learnt this way, and we won't overcome racism in society if we continue to deny each other the opportunity to learn. Imagine instead saying: 'What you said or did appeared racist. Are you willing for me to explain to you why?' Or at least asking the person to explain their action and what was going through their mind. But people simply condemn someone, without consideration, to the racist pool.

While the general yardstick should be that everyone must be treated with respect, we ought to take people on a learning experience rather than condemning them to the flames of hell. There is a kind, compassionate way of addressing things.

Having said that, we can no longer simply be bystanders in the fight against racism. We need to address the ticking time bomb in society. Nothing happens in between scandals. We retreat to corners to lick our wounds and learn absolutely nothing. Abuse thrives in silence. We become bland, too scared to voice our opinion out of fear for our own human frailties being exposed. And in their self-imposed silence, people harbour hate and resentment if there is no intervention.

What I've learnt is that intention matters, and that those who know your heart will never question your intentions. To pretend to be holier than thou or to think you'll never make a mistake is arrogant. While racism should be abhorred in all shapes and forms – from structural racism to the more subtle micro-aggressions accompanied by 'I didn't mean it that way' excuses – our intention should always be to learn and teach rather than to destroy.

During question time after a speaking engagement in Cape Town, a young black woman asked whether I ever censored myself and if I ever used the K-word (she actually used the word). I felt the hair on my arms stand up as she said it. I told her that I couldn't ever remember using the word. It's not used in my presence, and I despise it, no matter who says it. I don't have to censor myself at any point. People around me know that I don't tolerate the use of the word in my environment, and her mentioning it was the first time I'd heard it in several years. It was deeply upsetting, even being used by a black person.

It reminded me of the powerful TED talk 'The danger of a single story' by the Nigerian author Chimamanda Ngozi Adichie. It's about making blanket assumptions about any group or people, and how it is a sign of a lack of empathy and insight to ascribe conformist behaviour to a group of people when your experiences are limited to one or two interactions. Truth be told, I wanted to tell the young woman in the audience that I found her question highly offensive, but at the same time I had to acknowledge that she, too, had been hurt by history. And that required my empathy, compassion and recognition of her lived experiences.

When I'm asked to speak about diversity, to help people become conscious of their thought processes and to highlight how we automatically slip into patterns of thinking, I usually show a simple word or job title on a screen and ask the audience to record whether they think of the gender and race of the person. The first is usually 'fighter pilot'. For most people, a white male comes to mind. I then show a picture of Mandisa Mfeka, South Africa's first black woman combat pilot. I use similar imagery to alert people to their unconscious bias.

In 2023, I was invited to speak at a university in Medellín, Colombia. Having religiously watched the *Narcos* drama series on Netflix, I expected to be confronted by a similar reality. Whenever I told someone that I was travelling to Colombia, their response, without exception, was to caution me about safety. Once I was there, the first time I was asked whether I'd been to Colombia before, I foolishly offered information about my experiences as a Netflix viewer and expressed my curiosity about the drug trade and cartels. Very diplomatically, I was told that it was not something the Colombian people liked to reference as it represented a painful past. I saw the parallel with not wanting my own country's painful past to be the only point of reference about South Africa. I recognised my unconscious bias.

I had the most wonderful seven days exploring Medellín and another city, Cúcuta, close to the border with Venezuela. Colombia is one of the most beautiful countries I've visited, but the people impressed me even more. They expressed so much care and love that I felt at home. Apart from visiting one or two sites in remembrance of the people killed in the cartel wars, I had no sense of Medellín being the so-called drug capital of the world. I returned to South Africa realising that I, too, had bought into the 'single story'. No country is a Netflix series. No people are only what you see about them on TV. We must constantly remind ourselves that what we see and believe must be interrogated from all angles – and often experienced – before we can form an opinion.

Madiba said, 'I detest racialism, because I regard it as a barbaric thing, whether it comes from a black man or a white man.' I like to juxtapose these words with those of novelist Charles Dickens: 'Have a heart that never hardens, and a temper that never tires, and a touch that never hurts.'

If we can draw on Madiba's sense of justice, applied with compassion and forgiveness like he did, we can move forward knowing that our common purpose is for the good of all.

In conflict, neither side can claim victory

One of the most important lessons I have learnt in my life of struggle for freedom and peace is that in any conflict there comes a point when neither side can claim to be right and the other wrong, no matter how much that might have been the case at the start of a conflict.

– *Nelson Mandela by Himself: The Authorised Book of Quotations*, p 54

Managing conflict is so difficult. I avoid it as much as possible; it serves no purpose in my life and merely ends up consuming my thoughts and energy for endless periods. It's only in the past few years that I've managed to detach myself from a situation completely instead of engaging in conflict whenever possible (hence my occasional prolonged absence from social media). If it's something I feel strongly about and I can see that not speaking up will contribute to suffering, I still ask myself: will me telling my side of the story contribute to anyone feeling better or feeling worse?

Sometimes, when I read something on social media, I'm tempted to say things that I think need to be said about a person or a situation. But I often draft a message, delete it and then draft another – and, in the time it takes me to reflect on my words and feelings, I convince myself that my opinion on the matter isn't necessary and won't be helpful. There's a subtle difference between this approach and censoring ourselves because we fear the consequences of speaking out when it's important to do so.

Once, during an interview with Oprah Winfrey, Madiba said, 'I have taken insults from people I could destroy in one sentence, but I have kept quiet. If I have commented it was to praise them for their bravery to express their views no matter who was involved.'

Madiba made choices in his life not to serve only the interests of a select group; he made choices in the best interests of everyone. These were choices that had an impact on the fundamentals of life: where you could live, who you could love, how you could worship and who you could vote for. He deliberately chose peace over conflict to bring people together. He understood that neither side could win when there was conflict, and that the pain and suffering of a civil war would have been a burden for both sides to carry: the losers and the winners.

Throughout his life, Madiba maintained that the only solution to conflict was peaceful negotiations. He made it clear that when the apartheid government used force to stay in power and suppress the majority of South Africans, the ANC had no choice but to respond with force. He saw it, therefore, as a defensive, not an offensive, tactic. In 1999, President Mbeki asked Madiba to facilitate the Burundi peace negotiations and, as Madiba prepared for his role, I saw his unshakeable belief in the process. His goal was to broker peace between the Burundian government and the country's various rebel groups, notably the Forces for the Defence of Democracy as well as the National Forces of Liberation.

During the talks, we often visited Arusha, a beautiful town at the foot of Mount Kilimanjaro on the Tanzanian side. Meetings would sometimes last for days, and it felt as if the world outside stood still. Not one meeting concluded without Madiba stressing that ordinary people wanted peace and that it was any prospective leader's responsibility to work towards that. Outside the tense meeting venues, life continued as usual for the Tanzanian people, at a slow pace and in peace. It was as if Madiba took that feeling into the meeting rooms; he created the sense that the people trapped in negotiations were all leaders, without exception, and that their contributions and partici- pation were of cardinal importance no matter who they were. He may have elevated some people's importance by doing that, but it had the effect of making them invested in the process and the outcomes.

At times, I felt Madiba was coercing people into buying into his peaceful settlement, but in reality a firm hand was needed when it was clear that some parties were delaying the conclusion of a peace deal. In a way, Madiba made every person feel responsible for the many lives lost as conflict continued to rage on the outskirts of Bujumbura, the largest city in Burundi. Each delegate received a stipend for every day that negotiations were prolonged, which meant they felt no urgency to bring the matter to a close. This was not a matter Madiba ever raised because he wanted the negotiating parties to feel that they were people of integrity. But a good leader knows when it's time to force someone's hand. Intuition, or being able to read the room, is important in such situations. Madiba would be patient up to a point, but when he adopted a more serious tone and adjusted his body language a little, people knew he'd reached the end of his patience.

Someone once told me the first word he intended to teach his daughter was not Mommy or Daddy but *compromise*. I thought that spoke volumes. We're generally so driven by the need to be right or seeing ourselves as David bringing down Goliath that we're unable to make space for nuances that may lead to compromise.

Madiba's legal training taught him that any deal was based on both parties feeling that they'd won when, in fact, they'd sacrificed something too. Focusing on the winning rather than the losing softens the pain of the compromise. And you simply don't negotiate if you're not willing to compromise, because that's the nature of negotiations.

Leading in conflict required Madiba to have a strategic vision. He could see beyond immediate challenges and obstacles. He set out clear and achievable goals and communicated them in simple and understandable terms to all his followers.

When the popular ANC leader Chris Hani was murdered over Easter in 1993, Madiba went on national TV to appeal for calm in the country. It was a year before the first democratic elections. Had he not brought his followers back to focusing on the now-achievable goal – a new dispensation and democracy for all – that tragic event could have derailed the vision. Madiba saw beyond the immediate crisis and realised how volatile the situation was. He appealed to his supporters and critics alike by offering a balanced view on the situation, highlighting that while it may have been a white man who'd shot and killed Hani, it was an Afrikaans white woman who'd called in the registration number of the car in which Hani's assailants had made their getaway.

To lead in conflict, one must also build important alliances. Madiba was particularly good at that. As current South African politicians grapple with the concept of coalitions, it's useful to look at Madiba's leadership style for guidance on how to build effective partnerships. He cultivated partners across borders and at important institutions across the world. These alliances represented people from all walks of life, yet he had the ability to build bridges between groups and created a sense of shared purpose and solidarity by clearly communicating the benefits of his vision. He also truly believed that listening – even to dissidents – could lead you to new conclusions and add value to a process, often presenting solutions you may not have thought of yourself.

When Madiba appointed Trevor Manuel as finance minister in his cabinet, he consulted across the board, calling the heads of the major banks, business leaders and other groupings to get their input before announcing the appointment publicly. It was not merely to get the important decision rubber-stamped by these parties but also to allow them to feel part of the future.

No longer having a shared purpose or feeling of solidarity is greatly missed in South African society today. People feel solidarity in brief moments, such as when one of our sports teams achieves success. But, largely due to populism, divisiveness, discrimination and corruption, our leaders have been unable to move us towards a common goal, and we've lost our moral compass. Individuals serving in the most hallowed institutions in the three arms of the state – the executive (cabinet), the legislature (Parliament) and the judiciary (the courts of law) – have been compromised due to corruption, fraud, mismanagement or indifference. And when there's so much wrongdoing to point a finger at, it's difficult to restore trust in institutions that are expected to be above reproach.

When news broke in 2021 of then Minister of Health Dr Zweli Mkhize being complicit in tender irregularities involving a communications firm acting on behalf of the Department of Health during the Covid-19 pandemic, I was devastated. I thought I knew Zweli quite well and could never have imagined him being implicated in something such as this. At the same time, I'm aware that in politics, the truth is never freely available; to date, he has not been formally charged and there's no way of telling how much political meddling was at play in the whole saga. We know today that our intelligence services have, on occasion, been used for political gain, notably when President Mbeki was ousted from office. Then, once Zuma was in situ, the intelligence services were used to aid corruption.

Even before Madiba's death, I could see signs that all was not as it seemed. During his final days and weeks, I had grave suspicions that strategically-placed nurses had been deployed in his home by his own party to 'attend' to his medical needs. Can you imagine liberating your people and then being spied on while gravely ill, by the very same people you liberated? I guess we'll never know if my instincts were correct, and if so, who was responsible.

Actions have consequences

*Those who conduct themselves with morality, integrity
and consistency need not fear the forces of inhumanity
and cruelty.*

– *Nelson Mandela by Himself: The Authorised Book of Quotations*, p 121

The apartheid government offered Madiba freedom from incarceration six times. Of course there were always conditions attached. Each time, he rejected the offers and refused to compromise on his principles. When he walked to freedom on 11 February 1990, he forgave his oppressors and, going beyond what could be expected of someone who'd been imprisoned for 27 years, he went on to reconcile people from across the political spectrum. He always respected the rule of law, even when the racist and discriminatory apartheid laws resulted in court proceedings, and he built strong institutions during his presidency to create a legal system that would serve all South Africans. He was a selfless man who fought for the rights of all, regardless of their race or background.

Madiba believed in the inherent dignity of all human beings and worked to ensure that everyone was treated with respect and equality. Above all, he remained humble despite his great personal achievements. He always deflected praise that was directed at him to the collective. He led decisively, always holding on to his principles, even in insignificant tasks. To my mind, he embodied integrity, the quality of being honest and sticking to strong moral principles.

I'm often asked what I think Madiba would say about the levels of corruption in South Africa. The question has made me look beyond the cases that make headlines to explore the seeds of corruption that have become rooted in our society.

Corruption is not just a crime. It's a social crime, and it's particularly distressing that it's a scourge here, in one of the most unequal countries in the world, because it's the poorest citizens who indirectly suffer the most from its effects. On a macro scale, it affects stability, security and democracy. But corruption is not a new phenomenon that's emerged since the birth of our democracy. It is, in fact, one of South Africa's oldest 'traditions', something that has been part of political life for more than 350 years.

One only has to look at the inner workings of the Broederbond, the patronage of powerful and influential white Afrikaans men that only advanced those affiliated with their secret society, to understand that corruption has been part of our society for a long time. The Muldergate or Information scandal led to the resignation of Prime Minister John Vorster after it was found that he, together with cabinet minister Dr Connie Mulder, diverted $72 million from the defence budget to use it as a secret slush fund to pay for private holidays for their families, buy and register properties in their personal names, and even establish *The Citizen* newspaper to propagate the National Party cause and counter negative perceptions about apartheid.

In 1991 the Pickard Commission of Inquiry found that fictitious tenders and awarding of contracts to family members, as well as accepting lucrative gifts in return for contracts, and payments to companies for work and materials never delivered, were becoming the norm within the National Party's Department of Development Aid. According to the Pickard report a contract of R84 000 was exceeded by R1,1 million. The Tender board estimated the purchase of portable toilets to cost R2 million, but it was increased to R14 million without referral back to the board. The proceeds were diverted to a company owned by the two officials who prepared the tender. The company then went on to sell these toilets to the Department of Development Aid. These are just a few examples of corruption and fraud during apartheid. To deny its existence before the ANC took power is either ignorant or disingenuous.

Corruption doesn't discriminate or occur exclusively among black or white, rich or poor. When you enrich yourself or your friends and family through economic favours, or bestow a special privilege to benefit someone unfairly, even a stranger, it can be categorised as corruption.

A few years ago, I had a small apartment in Sea Point on Cape Town's Atlantic seaboard. I wanted to have shelves and lockable cupboards installed and, through an attorney I knew in the city, received a reference for a handyman. A friendly man came to take measurements and, while he was busy, asked a lot of questions about my time working for Madiba. I felt at ease because, based on his reference, I knew the man would do an honest job. He sent me a quote and I accepted it without even asking about the terms of payment; I was prepared to pay most of the sum upfront so he could buy the shelves and other materials. I only withheld a minimal amount to be paid on completion of the task.

About three days later, I asked about the installation date as I had travel plans the following week and wanted the shelves installed before I left. Originally, he'd indicated that the job would be done in the same week. He then told me he couldn't find any ready-made shelving in Cape Town and talked me through all the places he'd tried. We ended the call with him undertaking to look around some more. After a few hours, he called to say he'd found shelves but that they were earmarked for another job; if I paid the supplier a few extra bucks, it could convince him to redirect the shelves to me.

I was livid. This was a sign of how bribery, dishonesty and corruption had manifested in society on all levels. I refused to pay the extra money and told the handyman that if the shelves were not installed before the end of the week, I would report him to the attorney who'd suggested I use his services and tell him what kind of business he was running. I refused to become part of the endemic culture where everything got fixed with 'a few extra bucks'.

On another occasion, I was pulled over by traffic cops for not bringing my car to a complete standstill at a stop street. It was a hot summer's afternoon, and I was eager to get home to disappear into the coolness of my house. You immediately get a fright when stopped by a traffic cop. I was brought up to always respect authority, and this is still very present in my life. I was in the wrong and deserved to be fined. I opened my car window as the cop approached. He asked for my driver's licence, which I handed to him. I immediately said that I realised I hadn't stopped at the stop street and apologised. He looked at me and said, 'No, no, no, I'll have to fine you now,' meaning that he would have to issue me with a traffic-offence fine. I simply said, 'Yes, I understand,' and waited for him to take out his book to start writing up my details. But he then offered me an 'out' saying, 'But we can make this go away.' I felt my blood begin to boil – not from the heat outside but from rage. 'Excuse me?' was all I could muster. He said, 'Maybe you have something for me to buy a meal or a cooldrink.' I replied, 'No, please write me the ticket.' If he did, I'd have his details to report him, but he simply refused to take out his book to write the ticket. I insisted and an argument ensued. Unfortunately, this happened at a time before smartphones and I couldn't take a photo of him, something which, in later years, people have done when reporting corrupt traffic officials. He refused to write the ticket, and I refused to bribe him. After some time, he said, 'Well, you go off and don't skip the stop sign again.' I left it at that and thought that if I reported him, the cops would harass me. I was in the wrong, too, for not reporting the matter and allowing bribery or corruption to continue when I knew that the problem would not be solved unless we all took responsibility.

Corruption has been part of our landscape since the time of Jan van Riebeeck. He was banished to the Cape as his 'second chance' after being fired for using his office as head of a trading post in French Indochina (today known as Vietnam) to benefit personally. The period that followed, while Van Riebeeck and co. were establishing themselves at the Cape, was marked by tax evasion. During apartheid, those in power abused public funds too, to protect and further their own interests via the state coffers.

People love to argue now that corruption is more prevalent in government and with taxpayers' money – as I did during my Twitter fiasco. But it exists on every level of society, and we're so used to its occurrence that we've become desensitised to its presence in everyday life.

Sadly, even some of those whose job it is to enforce the law in South Africa have opened themselves up to bribery and corruption. A normal citizen who might on a regular day feel genuinely disgusted by corruption in politics and the public service could find themselves facing a moral dilemma. If they've somehow fallen foul of the law and are confronted by a police officer, the threat of having to spend a night in prison and the inconvenience of a criminal record, combined with the police's susceptibility to bribery, creates the perfect environment for small-scale corruption.

For example, I've heard of several cases in which a police docket opened after someone was charged with drunk driving had mysteriously disappeared. We should do everything in our power to remove this behaviour from society, even if it means we must pay the price. Tomorrow, that drunk driver may end up killing someone. I realise that if I insist on others not taking the easy way out of a sticky situation, I must abide by the same standards.

While the degeneration of many of our towns and cities can be directly linked to corruption at various levels of government, it's our inability to recognise or call out even the smallest act of dishonesty that has paved the way for those in power to keep lining their pockets with impunity.

On many occasions, Madiba expressed his opinion on the matter. As far back as 1998, in his address at the opening of the Morals Summit in Johannesburg, for example, he referred to corruption in both the public and private sector, 'where office and positions of responsibility are treated as opportunities for self-enrichment'.

After Madiba's retirement from public office in 1999, his delegation when travelling abroad was limited to a medical doctor, five security guards and me. The host country would supplement the security and provide the driver and, when venturing outside the hotel on business, we would usually leave two South African security guards behind to look after our rooms and belongings.

This was standard practice in all foreign countries, including on one of our visits to the Middle East. Our appointment with the head of state was late at night. Madiba was eager for us not to appear presumptuous, so we accepted the time slot given to us even though he'd reached the age where he preferred not to work at night.

We returned to the hotel after midnight, and I saw Madiba off for the night, assuming he would be eager to get to bed. In my hotel room, I checked my messages from home and was about to go to sleep when the phone in my room rang. (I always made sure Madiba had a list next to his bed with our room numbers and what numbers to dial in case he needed any of us during the night.) I thought it was one of the bodyguards or the doctor because I was convinced that Madiba had gone to bed already. When I answered, it was the angry voice of Madiba on the line that jolted me wide awake.

'Zelda,' he said. I immediately knew there was something wrong, as he rarely used my real name unless he was angry or irritated (he usually called me Zeldina). 'Come to my room.' At first, I thought he may have fallen or injured himself. I usually expect the worst – something I really hope I'll unlearn. As I rushed to his room, a million scenarios flashed through my mind. He knew it was well past midnight, so it must have been serious for him to call me to his room. The security guard in the room adjacent to his, with an interleading door, had to put on a robe to come and open the door to Madiba's suite for me.

Madiba was seated in the wingback chair in the lounge, next to the telephone, still wearing the clothes he'd selected for our meeting earlier that night. Some time had passed since I'd left him, and I thought it suspicious that he wasn't in his pyjamas; I also knew he was very tired, as midnight was well past his bedtime.

'Yes, Khulu,' I greeted him. I could see from his facial expression that he was furious.

'Call Jackie Selebi,' he said, pointing his index finger at the telephone. At the time, Selebi was South Africa's commissioner of police and the head of Interpol. It was now nearing 1 am and close to midnight back home. Not knowing why I would have to find Selebi, I asked: 'Khulu, why do you want me to call Jackie at this hour?'

'Just call him,' he answered, raising his voice a little. That was my cue to proceed with caution. Something had upset him terribly. Remembering that I'd read something about the commissioner attending to a serious case over the past few days, I reminded Madiba of the incident and emphasised that it was close to midnight at home and that it might not be good idea to call him so late. Madiba would not budge, so I had to change tactics. 'Why are we calling Jackie so late, Khulu? What should I tell him when I find him?' It was how I should have started in the first instance. I thought that perhaps if he repeated out loud what was bothering him, he may realise that the matter didn't require immediate attention.

When we were travelling the world, hotels and hosts tried to impress Madiba with obscene amounts of alcohol, flowers, food and designer-brand toiletries. As we were in a Muslim country, his room was decorated with beautiful bouquets of flowers on every table, in addition to dates, sweets and a full complement of luxury toiletries in his bathroom.

When Madiba said, 'Someone stole something from my bathroom,' I didn't know that it had been stocked with luxury toiletries and jumped to the conclusion that he wanted to call the commissioner because either his own toiletries had been stolen or there was a big item missing. If you're going to wake the head of Interpol, I thought sarcastically, it was probably a mirror or even the bathtub that had been stolen. I knew very well that I should retreat a little and try to defuse the situation by gently asking for more information.

It was then that Madiba told me more. Before we'd left for the presidential palace, he'd counted all the toiletries in his bathroom. When he got back, something was missing. I offered a few examples of what may have been stolen from the collection of toiletries, and he got even angrier at me for questioning him. With irritation, he said, 'I don't know, it is probably a bar of soap,' but he cited with conviction the number of items there should have been. He had thoroughly counted and made sure that he was not making false allegations against anyone. I was astonished and again I stressed that I didn't think it was a good idea to call the commissioner of police in the middle of the night.

Thankfully, it looked as if the tension was easing. I'd been scared to share my honest opinion at first, but clearly it was the best policy. Madiba was never deaf to reasoning and knew all too well that people could sometimes react impulsively when angered.

He then explained that he wanted to call the commissioner as he wanted all his bodyguards fired, because someone in our delegation must have taken the item from his bathroom and could therefore not be trusted with his safety.

We all knew him well enough to know that he was serious when making such threats.

Nelson Mandela was a lawyer by training, and that night his hotel room became a courtroom where he stepped into the role of prosecutor without effort. He interrogated the security guards, as they were the only members of the delegation who had remained behind when we left for our meeting. To me, he said, 'You sit as a witness.' I was silently grateful that I was not considered a suspect, as his wrath was too much to bear. He explained that he still intended to call the commissioner the next morning and have all the members of his security team dismissed, but then offered an escape clause. He said that if the person replaced the item they'd taken, he would forgive and forget, but he would not have any thieves in his delegation. 'If I cannot trust you with my things, I cannot trust you with my life.' There was no grey area for him in that.

As the security team had direct access to his bedroom and bathroom, the person, or someone else, replaced the item during the night. The next morning, when I met Madiba for breakfast, he reported that it was no longer necessary to report the matter to police headquarters. Crisis averted. Selfishly, I was worried about travelling with him without any security if he'd had them all fired, or whether it would cause a delay in our travel plans to wait for a replacement team. I couldn't imagine the logistical nightmare it would cause.

We left the hotel that day and, as he was leaving his room, I passed through the bathroom and quickly scanned the lounge area for any items he may have forgotten. Madiba didn't have many belongings, but the things he had he valued and treasured; if we forgot anything in a hotel, it would cause another crisis en route. As I entered the bathroom, I saw the spectacular exhibition of luxury-brand goods all unopened and unused.

I was curious why he'd made such a fuss over the stolen item if he had no intention of taking or using any of the items himself. 'No, you see,' he said, when I questioned him on the aeroplane, 'when your hosts show you such hospitality, you don't take things for granted. You want to leave a message that you know their wealth but that your intention is not to exploit them.' Thus it was better to leave everything behind. I immediately confessed that I always took the shower caps from hotel rooms, and he laughed at me, saying that if you needed the item, you were in your rights to use it or take it, but he didn't need any of the items.

I thought about it a lot. I didn't need the shower caps, but they really were convenient items to travel with and to have on hand in case you forgot your own. Madiba's own humility also prevented him from stating that his bathroom was obviously stocked in excess because of who he was.

He was completely intolerant of dishonesty in whichever way it presented itself.

So, when I'm asked about his feelings and thoughts on corruption in South Africa, I usually offer the story about the stolen 'bar of soap or something' and invite the audience to decide for themselves what he would have said about corruption.

I'm also often asked why he supported Jacob Zuma in his quest for public office. Of course, one must remember that when people presented themselves to Nelson Mandela, they would always show him their best side.

In around November 2011, Madiba and I were in Qunu, where he was at last enjoying his well-deserved retirement. From the start of that year, he'd been in and out of hospital due to a recurring infection. His health had deteriorated significantly but he still had some clarity and was comfortable and not in any pain. He could still move around and enjoyed the odd visitor when he was having a good day.

One such day was when then President Jacob Zuma travelled to Qunu to visit Madiba and report on the death of Libya's Brotherly Leader Muammar Gaddafi, who had been killed in October. Madiba had forged a friendship with Gaddafi when, just three months before retiring from the presidency in 1999, he negotiated – through the intermediaries Prof Jakes Gerwel and Prince Bandar bin Sultan Al Saud – for the Libyan leader to hand over the suspects of the 1988 Lockerbie bombing, which had killed hundreds of people aboard a plane flying over the Scottish town, as well as some of its residents. Madiba considered Gaddafi a man of his word because he'd delivered on his promise to surrender the two suspects, who were tried by a specially convened Scottish court of law in the Netherlands and sentenced to life imprisonment. Gaddafi also paid reparations to the families of those killed in the bombing.

Many things have been and will be said about Gaddafi, but given their history, it was a particularly sad event for Madiba to watch an ally being killed in cold blood on live TV, his body dragged through the streets for the world to see.

When President Zuma came to Qunu, it was to report on intelligence he'd received about Gaddafi's killing. He spent the morning with Madiba in his breakfast room, from where you could see the N2 and adjacent dirt road that ran parallel to the national highway. Outside, several VIP cars from the president's convoy were parked on Madiba's property. There were an impressive number of German luxury vehicles – quite the opposite to what we were used to. I was reminded how, during Madiba's presidency, I'd added my voice to the battle to convince someone to allocate extra money from their budget to the Presidential Protection Unit so they could buy decent and uniform cars for Madiba's convoy. But Madiba had protested, saying there was no money for luxury and that every cent at the government's disposal should be used to improve the lives of impoverished people.

During breakfast, Madiba got distracted by something and said, 'JZ [using the president's initials], where did you get that watch?'

'Eh he he,' laughed Zuma in his characteristic way. He was wearing a massive gold watch with a square face that covered the width of his arm. It was hard not to notice. The president pulled his sleeve over it and said, 'No, Tata [father in isiXhosa], it was a gift.'

Madiba continued his breakfast – or rather kept moving food around on his plate as he had little appetite left at his age – and listened intently to the report of events in Libya. After a while, one of the cars outside moved, catching Madiba's attention. He said, 'Man, JZ, whose cars are those?'

'Eh he he,' he laughed again. 'Tata, those are the cars of the presidential convoy.'

'Oh, I see,' Madiba answered. Not five minutes later, he again asked, 'JZ, man, where did you get that watch?' Zuma looked at me, and I repeated what he'd said earlier – that he'd received it as a gift. When Madiba asked for the third time, I really knew that something was bothering him. I interjected and kindly reminded Madiba that he'd asked the same question a few times. He left the matter at that and returned to pushing food around on his plate.

Once I'd blocked that line of questioning, Madiba turned his attention to the cars again. I reminded him that JZ was the president and that he was entitled to a convoy, upon which Madiba expressed his disapproval of such an ostentatious show of power.

The truth is that Madiba was always worried when public servants lived ostentatiously. A president or anyone else in public office should not flaunt luxury cars, expensive jewellery and clothes.

Madiba often said the former president and dictator of Zimbabwe, Robert Mugabe, drove everywhere with a large convoy because he was insecure. Somehow, the practice became a president's status symbol: the more cars and the flashier they are, the more powerful the leader.

There was nothing untoward about receiving a watch as a gift. On many occasions Madiba had received watches from overseas hosts too. The problem was that a sitting president had to report all donations and gifts, according to what is known as the Ministerial Handbook, and rumours were already doing the rounds about corruption in government involving Zuma. Even so, the gift was not the problem but rather the expectations accompanying it. It was clear that Madiba's intuition was warning him that something was amiss, years before the Public Protector issued the State Capture Report that exposed government corruption on a massive scale.

In *Good Morning, Mr Mandela*, I documented how obsessed Madiba became with Zuma's relationship with Schabir Shaik, who in 2005 was sentenced to fifteen years in prison for corruption and fraud. Madiba's intuition that Zuma had been compromised was underpinned by his own standards of integrity and ethics. One can argue that we all know the difference between right and wrong, but in recent times some people have mastered the art of arguing – and even convincing themselves – that they deserve something, which justifies their crime.

In his Morals Summit address in 1998, Madiba said, 'Having come into government with the declared intention of eliminating the corruption we knew to be endemic, we have in the past four years found that some individuals who fought for freedom have also proved corrupt. Nor should our apartheid past be used as an excuse for such misdemeanours.'

While the ANC should accept responsibility for its complicity in the large-scale corruption that has directly prevented people from enjoying a better life as promised by the liberation movement, journalist and political commentator Sipho Masondo believes that the ANC would need to destroy itself first before it can be fixed. It's a sad situation.

I think of the 27 years Madiba was imprisoned and the effect it had on him. Like others who have expressed this thought, I believe Madiba would have had a much brighter future if he'd been younger when he was released. He sacrificed his freedom for the struggle and its people, but also for the survival of the ANC. Thus, to see it implode is painful and tantamount to the sacrifices that he and his comrades made being turned to dust.

Our contradictions
make us human

We are fragile creatures, and it is from this weakness, not despite it, that we discover the possibility of true joy. Life is filled with challenges and adversity. Fear is inevitable, as is pain and eventually death.

– Desmond Tutu, The Book of Joy

This insight by the Arch has prompted me to think more deeply about human nature, as has Madiba's observation, contained in a letter he wrote to medical doctor and activist Effie Schultz in 1987 when he was in Cape Town's Pollsmoor Prison: 'Contradictions are an essential part of life and never cease tearing one apart.' I guess I've come to realise that it's precisely our fragility and the unavoidable contradictions within ourselves that make us human.

The founder and leader of the mainly KwaZulu-Natal-based Inkatha Freedom Party (IFP), Prince Mangosuthu Gatsha Buthelezi, died in 2023. Before the 1994 elections, many white South Africans felt that if the country was destined to have a black president, they would prefer Buthelezi to Madiba because, while the latter was considered a hater of white people – a notion created by the apartheid propaganda machine – Buthelezi had appealed to whites to work together. Soon after I started working for Madiba, I met Dr Buthelezi and liked him; he appeared to be friendly, kind and respectful. At the time, he was serving in President

Mandela's cabinet as the minister of home affairs and often acted as president when both Madiba and Deputy President Mbeki were abroad. Most controversially, he was at the helm when the decision was made to send Southern African Development Community (SADC) troops from South Africa and Botswana to quell a Lesotho Defence Force (LDF) mutiny and widespread civilian unrest following the disputed 1998 election there. Diplomatic efforts had failed and, when the unrest spiralled out of control, Buthelezi called Madiba several times to garner support for a military intervention. Madiba and his delegation were in Mauritius for a SADC meeting before flying to the US. Every time Buthelezi called Madiba, he would in turn call Mbeki to consult. It was difficult to read the situation while they were abroad, so they largely relied on Buthelezi's assessment. The two men approved the military intervention in principle but left the final decision to Buthelezi. What unfolded was a bloody confrontation in which nine South African soldiers died, as well as more than three times as many LDF members and at least 47 Basotho civilians. Although the intervention eventually led to the formation of an inclusive Independent Political Authority, the military invasion was largely seen as an overreaction and an embarrassment for the South African government.

This altered my opinion of Buthelezi to some extent. Still, I generally liked him, and Madiba was always amused by my imitation of him. When Dr Buthelezi died in 2023, I was sad as it signified the end of an era with another of the old guard departing. But my limited views on him were based on my interactions and what I've described. It was only when I read opinion pieces written by Mondli Makhanya and John Carlin, two journalists whose views I regularly use as a yardstick for my own opinions, that I really got a sense of the Buthelezi that I didn't know in the 1980s.

I remember hearing as a teenager about the endless battle between the ANC and the IFP and violent attacks on hostels as they fought for the soul of KwaZulu-Natal. I read each word of the two opinion pieces, almost with disbelief. Buthelezi's death and the differing views on his legacy made me realise how much we still had to learn as South Africans. Google only started gaining traction in 1999–2000, and South African history probably made it onto the search engine in the mid-2000s. So what we knew then was based on what we'd read in newspapers during the 1980s and 1990s, censored or not. I'd completely lost sight of people's lived experience of the brutality of Buthelezi's death squads. In an article that appeared in *City Press* after Buthelezi's death in September 2023, Mondli, editor of the newspaper, wrote:

> The carnage of those times was raw: people butchered in broad daylight, babies stabbed with spears while in bed with their mothers because 'a baby snake will eventually grow up into a big snake' . . .
>
> The sight of severed limbs, heads separated from the torsos, and congealed blood thick on the floors of homes and streets still haunts to this day.

I'd made the same mistake as I did with my views on Jan van Riebeeck. Dr Buthelezi's legacy is much more complex than simply that of a willing and able leader who worked alongside Madiba at the dawn of democracy. Our experiences are one-sided, subjective and grossly flawed at best.

In 1996, Madiba shielded Dr Nkosazana Dlamini-Zuma, then minister of health and one of Jacob Zuma's former wives, after she had not followed government contract procedure and had overpaid for the stage play *Sarafina*, which was designed to convey a safe-sex message to communities that didn't have access to mainstream media. Many people point to this as the start of the era of corruption in South Africa. It's not an unfair criticism. As much as I loved Madiba, his failure to act against his minister in this instance was a major mistake in his presidency.

And then, two years later, came the infamous arms procurement deal. Controversially, it was alleged that the Nelson Mandela Children's Fund

(NMCF), the first charity that Madiba started during his presidency, had received a donation of R500 000 when the deal was negotiated. I'll never forget that day: all hell broke loose in our office. Madiba summoned the CEO, Sibongile Mkhabela, and instructed her to find out if it was true, and if so, to return the donation immediately.

Two years into his presidency, Madiba announced that he would serve for only one term and that he was leaving the running of the country to Deputy President Mbeki. Negotiations around the provisions of the arms deal were therefore left to members of Madiba's cabinet, and he was mainly briefed by Defence Minister Joe Modise. Madiba often said that if you questioned a person's integrity without valid reason, it could well reflect your own integrity. I'm certain that no minister entered his office to come and report corruption or fraud.

In July 2021, Zuma's legal team wrote to the Nelson Mandela Foundation and the ANC to obtain financial records from them about donations. It appears as if they wanted to involve Madiba in the arms deal by trying to prove that he, too, had accepted money. The arms deal was concluded between 1998 and 1999. In May 1999, Madiba retired from public office. Three months later, we started the Nelson Mandela Foundation with a R1 million loan to launch our offices and operations because there was no funding available from the government, or any other quarter, for a post-presidential office. I assume that we would not have spent weeks worrying about funds to run the office if there had been any such donations from the arms deal. What I know is that Madiba did not tolerate dishonesty in his immediate circle. If he had been aware of corruption or fraud around the arms deal, he would have acted on it.

He would always give people the benefit of the doubt and encourage them, through his trust in them, to do the right thing. Unfortunately, it seems that some people took advantage of that goodwill. In his later years, Madiba was gravely concerned about dishonesty, fraud and corruption in government, and he would get so upset by it that we sometimes hid the newspapers from him.

On many occasions, he refused favours and gifts when he believed there would be expectations from the donor. He went to great lengths to explain to potential donors that there could not be an expectation of him as president to return any favours.

I recall one incident after his retirement when I was unable to find a private aeroplane for him to travel to Cape Town. I resorted to asking a wealthy and influential businessman to help. When we arrived at the airport, the businessman introduced Madiba to the owner of the plane. But something felt uncomfortable. The owner wanted to travel with us to Cape Town, so Madiba told the mutual friend that we would cancel our trip.

When South Africa set its sights on hosting the 2010 Fifa World Cup, Madiba was instrumental in the success of the bid. A last-minute trip to Trinidad and Tobago to convince soccer administrators that South Africa was ready to host the event, as well as countless meetings at home and in Zurich, contributed to South Africa being announced the winner. Jack Warner, a Trinidadian and Tobagonian politician and football executive, was forced upon us by South Africa's bid committee. Much to the irritation of officials of the Nelson Mandela Foundation, me included, we were expected to bend over backwards to accommodate Warner's requests without following the normal procedures around Madiba that had been set up to protect him. Warner was later implicated in numerous corruption scandals and, in 2015, received a Fifa lifetime ban from football-related activities. In 2013, the American soccer administrator Chuck Blazer, someone we knew well because of our interactions with Fifa over the years and in the lead-up to the bid, admitted in a New York federal court to accepting bribes from both Morocco and South Africa for hosting rights. Both these individuals were close associates of Madiba in the years leading up to South Africa's successful bid. But was Madiba ever compromised? No. I was labelled 'difficult' because I questioned every aspect of the demands the bid committee and the Fifa officials made of us, especially the inexplicable, all-access privileges they enjoyed around Madiba. The stories of corruption and mismanagement that emerged, specifically involving Warner and Blazer, proved that my instinct, my uneasiness with the situation at the time, had been right. We were certainly not aware of private dealings with the officials, and I doubt that anyone would have shared details of bribes, corruption or money laundering with Madiba before such meetings took place.

It was only when the Netflix series *Fifa Uncovered* was aired that all the pieces of the puzzle began to fall into place. During a casual conversation with a former journalist who'd watched the documentary, she expressed her disappointment at Madiba's involvement in the corruption scandal. I was angered because merely by being the face of South Africa's World Cup bid, Madiba had been implicated in the scandal. It's simply not true that people in his position are always aware of others' underhand actions.

I look at my own behaviour through the lens of the lessons I learnt from these and other experiences. I, too, might have played a role in enabling dishonesty in certain instances. On a trip to England, we stayed at Douw Steyn's residence in the countryside while Madiba was on a fundraising trip for the Nelson Mandela Foundation. Douw had arranged to host several lunches and dinners with influential and wealthy people so Madiba could introduce them to the foundation and ask for support.

When we left, our luggage went with the advance team to the airport, where they checked us in ahead of our arrival. As the luggage went through an X-ray machine, the advance team officer saw that one of the suitcases had cutlery in it. He opened the luggage and found that it was the same cutlery used by our hosts. It was obvious that these pieces had been stolen.

The advance team officer called to let me know what he'd discovered and told me who the suitcase belonged to: one of the security officers in the Presidential Protection Unit. I had a choice: report it to Madiba, which would mean that the officer would be dismissed immediately, or report it to the individual's commanders back home and ask them to take appropriate action. I chose the latter because I knew the man had a wife and kids and, with a modest salary, couldn't afford to lose his job. He was demoted and moved out of the Presidential Protection Unit.

However, I realise that it's precisely such actions, or inactions such as mine, that have helped to create an environment in which corruption and fraud flourish in South Africa. Jon Ronson writes: 'The snowflake doesn't feel responsible for the avalanche.' Indeed, we don't think our individual actions contribute to the wider social reality in which we find ourselves.

How were my actions different from Madiba overlooking the *Sarafina* saga? We try to be gentle with people because we think our actions may cause pain – even if there's a valid reason for the action. But sadly, if we overlook, participate in or look away from any form of illegal activity, it does matter, as it contributes to undermining the moral fabric of society. We're never more righteous than when we're in the wrong, and we're all responsible for what we become as a society. Unless we all refuse to bribe a cop to let us off a traffic offence, and we say no to pirated movies and buying counterfeit luxury handbags and jewellery, we'll keep going on the road to becoming one of the most corrupt nations on earth. Each of us is responsible for the dysfunctional system. The 'yes but' crowd will say there are more serious crimes being committed. This may be true, but it is also a refusal to accept responsibility for our situation. People say, 'But I didn't vote for the ANC,' to try to abdicate responsibility for the trajectory our country is taking. But denying our role – active or passive – isn't helpful. It's true that we can't stop things from going wrong or the world from being bad, but we should never stop trying.

It's easier to change
others than yourself

One of the most difficult things is not to change society –
but to change yourself.

– Nelson Mandela by Himself: The Authorised Book of Quotations, p 45

Changing is a natural process and something we experience consistently throughout our lives. It shouldn't be difficult for us to adapt, yet it's one of our greatest challenges and many life-changing events are hugely traumatic. What I've learnt is that if we're able to adapt with greater ease, we can generally cope a lot better with the effects of change. And that begins with changing ourselves.

Democracies across the globe are challenged by complex issues relating to migration, the integration of immigrants and the changes this brings. It requires a fair amount of mindfulness, compassion and understanding to deal with these issues, and looking at them in the context of history can offer some insight.

We know that for centuries Europe colonised Africa, extracted wealth and exploited local people as labourers, stunting organic growth and development. Once countries gained independence, the effects of exploitation and oppression continued to reverberate through society long after the colonisers had gone, with a lack of education and experience contributing to slow growth. Fast forward to the present, where countries across the globe have been affected by fraud and corruption. This also has an impact on countries still reeling from the effects of colonisation. Add civil war and dictatorship, and you can begin to understand why many people want to explore better opportunities elsewhere. For many middle-class educated people around the world, it's fairly uncomplicated to uproot their lives and move elsewhere in search of a better life. People have been doing it for centuries. But for immigrants fleeing poverty, civil unrest and dictatorship, their options for a new home are limited to where they can – often illegally – enter without being detained or deported back to what they're trying to escape from. In South Africa, we've seen an influx of immigrants from countries north of us, especially Zimbabwe, Malawi and Mozambique. Within the borders of our own country, semigration takes place constantly, with people moving to the main cities in search of work or to areas offering better service delivery and safety.

Democracies all over the world have spectacularly failed at implementing immigration policies that work for both citizens and immigrants. But, because of the difficulties around integration, people have turned it into a personal issue and racism has raised its head, driving us further apart. My own experience of semigrating from Gauteng to the Cape a few years ago and the challenges it brought gave me valuable insight into the complexities involved. It seems hypocritical for people to criticise those who migrate in search of better opportunities in other countries when we do so within our own country too.

Changing circumstances were part of Madiba's life from an early age, and he was a migrant at various stages of his life. The lessons we can draw from how he dealt with this are universal, whether you're a migrant of some sort or a sedens – still living in the place or region of your birth. Although there is disagreement about how old Madiba was when his father died – some sources say nine, others twelve – it was undoubtedly his first massive life-changing event. He looked up to his father, and his death left his mother in dire poverty trying to fend for herself and her children. The young Madiba had grown up considering his father to be an important figure, not only in the house as the head of the family but also in terms of tribal affairs. Madiba's father, Nkosi (Chief) Mphakanyiswa Gadla Henry Mandela, was a senior counsellor to the Thembu regent. He was a tall, stately figure, and the young boy idolised him. From Madiba's retelling of the story, I got a sense that the period before his father's passing was considered a time of progress and stability. He often recounted how he was born to royalty, and when visiting Queen Elizabeth II of Britain, he would remind her that he, too, had royal blood.

The death of his father must have left him reeling.

The next major shift in Madiba's young life happened only a few months after his father's death. He was sent to be cared for by the regent, Chief Jongintaba. He told me how he and his mother had left at dawn one morning to walk to the 'Great Place', Mqhekezweni, where the chief lived, some 30 kilometres from their home in Qunu. The journey was imprinted in his mind as a sad affair, probably with an uncertain future looming as they crossed the vast, picturesque landscape of rolling hills. Every step was a step closer to uncertainty. He remembered that he and his mother didn't talk much during the journey and that it took an entire day to reach their destination.

At the regent's compound, he was first introduced to a western-style building, a house with a corrugated iron roof and right-angled corners, different from the traditional rondavels he knew. There was no running water or electricity, but to him, the buildings, the consistent food provisions, the presence of a car and being able to freely roam the hills surrounding the Great Place, appeared luxurious. This environment, and the education he received, offered the young Madiba an aristocratic sophistication compared with the poverty at his mother's house. Later in life, he wrote that it was only when he was imprisoned that he truly understood the depth of the poverty in which his mother had been left after his father's death.

Madiba was sent to a Methodist boarding school called Clarkebury in Engcobo in the Eastern Cape. He only returned to the Great Place over long school holidays and rarely saw his mother, although as an adult he acknowledged that she'd been his first 'best friend'. A mother is how we come to be here and what grounds us to this life. A separation like this must have been devastating.

From a young age, the young Rolihlahla, who'd been given the 'Christian' name Nelson by his teacher, Miss Mdingane, when he was at primary school in Qunu, was considered different from other children. He exhibited leadership qualities, always being the more responsible of the boys, obedient most of the time and working hard to adjust to his surroundings.

It was during his secondary years of schooling in Healdtown that he first encountered other cultures – people from Swaziland and Lesotho, for example. He said the experience and exposure 'loosened the hold of tribalism that imprisoned me'. For many years during his presidential term and in retirement, he warned of the dangers of tribalism in our democratic state. One only has to look at the history of countries such as Rwanda, where there was a bloody civil war between Hutus and Tutsis, to see the dangers of tribalism.

We can't function in isolation from others. In trying to understand the world we live in, I've always felt that it's important to understand other cultures and traditions that surround us, and to make this part of adapting to the changing environments throughout our lives. During my time with Madiba, I learnt so many interesting things about other cultures. We have such rich diversity in South Africa to learn from. To make people comfortable with change, I always advise corporate clients to have cultural days once a month during which people from a particular cultural heritage get to share their traditions, food preferences and a taste of their history. I feel that experiencing something gives us a better understanding of it and helps us recognise how diversity can enrich our lives.

The next major life change for Madiba was when he was expelled from the University of Fort Hare for opposing the Student Representative Council election process and declining to serve unless the body was given more powers to deal with issues such as the quality of food served to students.

Being at the university campus during the filming of our six-part documentary series on the people and places that influenced Nelson Mandela took me back to a bygone era. When you walk around at the university, the history associated with it is tangible. I could well imagine the young Madiba organising a protest, and it wasn't hard to visualise how they crouched around the only wireless radio in the dormitory to listen to news about the impending war in Europe. I could see Madiba walking around the grounds of the university, a handsome young man, always stoic and dressed impeccably, and meeting the young Oliver Tambo on the soccer pitch, where they first interacted. While studying documents in the university's archives, we came across an interesting discovery. When Madiba first enrolled at Fort Hare, he incorrectly wrote his birth date in the register as 18/06/1918 instead of 18/07/1918. It may have been a simple human error, but for me it pointed to a time when he was less meticulous and a little more careless. It was a welcome discovery.

When Madiba returned to Mqhekezweni, the regent was furious to learn of his expulsion. Soon after, the regent announced that he'd identified a wife for his own son Justice and one for young Nelson Mandela. At this point, Madiba realised that the only way to secure a future with possibilities was to defy the regent and run away. Justice joined him and, as described earlier, they got a lift to Johannesburg. There they secured jobs at a mine because of Justice being related to the regent, but when Chief Jongintaba learnt about this, he instructed the mining bosses to fire them. Madiba managed to find accommodation in Alexandra, one of the poorest informal settlements in South Africa – yet another major change for the young man. In Alexandra, he rented a back room at the simple house of an acquaintance and started his articles at a law firm in Johannesburg. His accommodation was about twenty kilometres from where he worked, and some weeks he simply didn't have money for transport so he would set off on foot well before dawn to arrive on time at the legal practice. He knew hardship but, through education and hard work, he was determined to break the cycle of poverty that entrapped his family.

Perhaps the most dramatic change Madiba had to face was being in prison and constantly confronted with changing circumstances there, too. It was painful to be cut off from his family and loved ones. To make this worse, the authorities used basic privileges such as correspondence and visits – or withholding these – as a means of punishment to undermine the inmates' mental state. Yet, in a letter to his wife, Winnie, on 23 June 1969, Madiba wrote: 'Hope is a powerful weapon.' In today's world of instant communication via the technology we have at our fingertips, it's hard to imagine what it must have felt like to be allowed to write only one letter from prison every six months – a letter that was then heavily censored.

Constant change throughout Madiba's life meant he had to keep adapting. Even later in his life, I saw how changing circumstances affected his ways.

Madiba realised that change made people uneasy – although he knew from first-hand experience that we were highly adaptable beings. Still, he saw no need to make people uneasy. If he put them at ease, they would perform better.

As is well documented now, shortly after taking office in 1994, he called staff together at his offices and residences to allay their fears about the new administration. I was not part of the office then, but I was told that people were nervous when they were summoned by the president. They were all expecting to be fired on the spot because they represented the previous regime. However, he told people that they would not be expected to leave unless they wanted to. The office would be changing, but he wanted to give them the opportunity to decide whether they wanted to be part of the new administration.

That set people at ease. Many later opted to take voluntary severance packages, but Madiba addressing the issue allowed them to make critical, life-changing decisions without added anxiety.

Whenever he met a particular cultural group in South Africa, he made sure that a staff member from the same cultural group was present. That's how people relate, and it adds a layer of confidence and the sense of belonging that I highlighted earlier. No matter how unpleasant the message was that he wanted to convey or how difficult the issue, Madiba made sure to create an environment conducive to dealing with the complexities.

A politician's job is to make the impossible possible. Madiba set out a goal to stabilise South Africa and establish democracy, and he did exactly that. The task of running a country is, however, an insatiable beast. There will always be more emphasis on one agenda than another, and I have no doubt that, to date, there hasn't been a president anywhere in the world who got everything right.

To soften the edge of change and to ensure a smooth handover to the new government, it was important to President Mandela to have interim representation of both old and new in important government departments.

Part of the social nature of human beings is our sense of connected-ness to others. Madiba applied this principle not only in smoothing the transition to democracy in South Africa but also in his dealings in other countries and contexts. Again his starting point was that familiarity put people at ease. If you create that environment for people who are experiencing change, they find it easier to adapt.

During the Burundi negotiations, for example, he impressed on delegates that an interim government should be completely represen-tative; there should be someone that every citizen of Burundi could identify with. People don't buy into change or solutions if they don't see themselves represented.

Although cadre deployment and land redistribution have failed due to ineffective implementation, the ideals are noble – to ensure that representation and socioeconomics change. We have high-calibre people of all races in South Africa. Our scientists, engineers and medical specialists, among others, compete with the best in the world. While transformation is an absolute necessity, we can't transform at the cost of weakening our key institutions. It's a fine balancing act but not impossible.

During my first winter in the Cape, I felt as if I'd made the biggest mistake of my life. The wind blew for three days without stopping, and it rained constantly. I felt as if I would go crazy being indoors for days on end; I was used to the sun being out on winter days up north. But you change and you adapt. The next year, I bought the appropriate clothing, and now I go out for my daily walk irrespective of the weather. It's a simple analogy, but when you move to a new place, you adapt to the weather – so why would you not also adapt to the culture and tradition of the place?

Those of us fortunate to travel abroad know that every city around the world is rich with tradition and its own culture. You do as the locals do. But for some inexplicable reason, many people feel that when they get to a new place, they have to change its tradition and culture to emulate what they're accustomed to. If newcomers try to impose their ways upon locals, conflict will ensue. But, as with most things, there are two sides to the coin: it's also incumbent on the long-time residents of a place, or the citizens of a particular country, to educate themselves and others about what migrants may find challenging in their new environment. Integration requires a measure of compromise, a willingness to reach across the divide and, as always, a generous amount of compassion and understanding on both sides, as well as honouring the principles of democracy.

Throughout Nelson Mandela's life, he lived by principle. Even in prison, being subjected to the rules of incarceration did not derail his

Even after Madiba's passing Mrs Machel continues to be part of my life and I have the privilege of spending quality time with her whenever we are able to. She remains my second mother and someone I love dearly and depend on for advice.

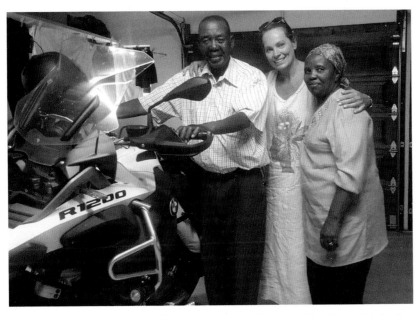

With Issau and Jogabeth Shilaluke, posing with my last motorbike. Jogabeth helped raise me and remains part of my life even though she is retired now. I credit most of my foundation in childhood to her hand in my upbringing.

The La Grange family in the town Cabriéres-d'Aigues in France's Luberon district. During our visit to the town we discovered the ship manifest which lists our first descendant, Pierre Grange, as a passenger leaving France for South Africa, as part of the French Huguenots fleeing persecution by the Catholics.

With my good friend Anele Mdoda who is always ready to support and counsel me.

Visiting Prof Jonathan Jansen and his family at their home in Bloemfontein
after the 2015 Twitter storm.

With General Bantu Holomisa and political analyst Prince Mashele
during the Zuma protests in 2021.

At the funeral of Madiba's friend and fellow prisoner, Ahmed Kathrada, with
Chief Mandla Mandela, George Bizos and Mrs Machel.

Ⅱ 220/82 : NELSON MANDELA .

POLLSMOOR MAXIMUM PRISON,
Private Bag X 4,
TOKAI   7966.
29.   8   83.

GESENSOR CENSORED   6
DATUM/DATE   83.08.30

Liewe Adele,

my kennis van Afrikaans is baie swak en my woordeskat laat veel te wense oor. Op my ouderdom sukkel ek nog om my grammatika aan te leer en my bewoording te verbeter. Dit sal seker rampspoedig wees as ek hierdie brief in Afrikaans skryf. Ek hoop van harte dat u sal verstaan as ek nou in Engels oorslaan.

Zami has told me several times of the interest you and Piet have shown in her problems over the past 6 years. Although I have on each occasion requested her to convey my appreciation to you, the beautiful and valuable present of books you sent me has given me the opportunity of writing to thank you directly for your efforts.

It was certainly not so easy for her at middle-age to leave her home and to start life in a new and strange environment and where she has no means of earning a livelihood. In this regard, the response of friends has, on the whole, been magnificent, and it made it possible for her to generate the inner strength to endure what she cannot avoid. We were particularly fortunate to be able to count on the friendship of a family that is right on the spot and to whom she can turn when faced with immediate problems. U en Piet tree het in 'n groot mate tot haar relatiewe veiligheid en geluk; I sincerely hope that one day I will be able to join you in your village and shake your hands very warmly as we chat along.

Part of the letter that Madiba wrote from prison in 1983 to express his gratitude to Piet and Adele de Waal for caring for Winnie while she was banished to Brandfort and placed under house arrest.

With Advocate Thuli Madonsela.

With the founder of 67 Blankets for Nelson Mandela Day, Carolyn Steyn, and PJ Powers during a blanket event in Pretoria.

The multi-party representation during a protest to Parliament in Cape Town to call for President Zuma's resignation.

After the publication of *Good Morning, Mr Mandela* I was invited to give a speech at the Clinton Presidential Center in Little Rock, Arkansas. Here I am with the Clinton Foundation organiser Yana-Janell Scott. To this day the Clintons still show an interest in my wellbeing and send birthday wishes every year.

principles. The lesson is that whatever the circumstances, whether you're a migrant or a local, your behaviour and your response to complex issues should be guided by your principles. Yes, it's the responsibility of governments to implement fair and appropriate policies, but it's up to each of us to shape society and influence those policies so that they serve the best interests of humanity.

On a personal level, I've witnessed how my story – my inclusion as an Afrikaner in Madiba's life – has helped people through change. I am humbled by it and use it to illustrate that we are all capable of the unthinkable. After I was appointed to my role in the Presidency, a documentary entitled *A Day in the Life of the President* was aired on national TV. On the day when the crew was filming, I happened to serve tea to the president and his guests. No job was ever too big or small for me, and I was happy to help. During filming, Jay Naidoo, the minister without portfolio in President Mandela's cabinet, was having a meeting with Madiba. In the documentary, I can be seen entering the office nervously to serve tea, and the president introducing me to Jay.

After the documentary was broadcast, my parents were told that friends of theirs had announced they couldn't be friends with the La Granges anymore because their daughter had served tea to a black man. On many occasions, I expressed my frustration to Madiba that people in my own community, the white Afrikaans community, weren't changing fast enough for my liking. I later realised that exposure was critical to change.

The comments by these so-called friends stuck. My parents were ostracised by them and some other 'friends', and it was unpleasant. Although at the time my parents still shared a political orientation with those people and hadn't yet changed their mindset – they were still clinging to apartheid nostalgia – it must have hurt them a great deal. But in a strange way, it started the process of change in their lives.

Yet, after the launch of *Good Morning, Mr Mandela* in 2014, I was doing a motivational talk for a financial institution. It was a voluntary session, an incentive for those who invested with this company. Following my talk, I sold books, signed copies and posed for photos with guests. When I looked up after signing a book, the family who'd made those comments about mine were standing in front of me. The magic of Nelson Mandela, I thought to myself. I smiled, pretending to be happy to see them, but in that moment I realised that by touching my life, Madiba had not only changed me, my family and those close to me, but even people like them. I saw the truth of his words about forcing people to change. He always told me *not* to force people, or the change would not be authentic.

This family had known exactly what my speech would be about: my life with Nelson Mandela. Clearly, they'd come around to wanting to hear more, perhaps to learn a little about Madiba; after all, no one had forced them to attend. Now they were standing in front of me, buying my book and wanting me to inscribe it. Although my inclination was not to engage with them, in that moment I was faced with the power of Madiba's legacy. The lessons I'd learnt came to the forefront, and I took time to talk to them and to write a beautiful message in their book.

It felt like a small victory. I don't know what their lives were like at home or how they acted in private, but the fact that they'd arrived and were at least open to listening showed the ripple effect of Madiba's influence on my life.

Many of my early friendships ended when I started working for Madiba. Some people came round and others didn't. Part of growing up for me was to accept that I simply could not change people. I can influence – we all have that ability – and, by not tolerating something like racism in my personal life, I feel that I can make a difference. It's not about forcing people to change but about dictating behaviour in your own environment. We all have rules within our social structures: what's acceptable to your group of friends and what not. It's true that I alienated many white Afrikaans people because of my stance on racism. According to some, you automatically become 'anti-white' if you stand up against racism, and sometimes if I'm in a restaurant or public place where white people traditionally gather, I feel like an imposter. I feel a loneliness I can't describe to anyone.

There's no political school or mass media campaign that teaches about racism. We all make judgements, and we all have micro-aggressions that we dump on others every day. When you're not thinking and you give someone you see at a traffic light a certain look, it has an impact on that person – it makes them feel small. For us to change takes effort. Think of how difficult it is to change our appearance or get rid of bad habits. We're impatient creatures. It requires compassion and empathy towards yourself and others to stimulate change. We all hate being told how to behave, but we can influence through our behaviour and actions while trying to remain unfazed by what might discourage us along the way.

The thing I heard Madiba say most often during the nineteen years I worked for him was that it was easier for him to change others than to change himself. He went into prison an angry and bitter man but realised that unless he got rid of his hatred and resentment, he could not preach reconciliation; he had to be reconciled with his own feelings first. He knew that darkness would only attract more darkness.

Madiba encouraged change as an exciting process of learning and developing, perhaps as he must have experienced it to some extent during his early years. Being so vocal about his intentions as a leader and preparing people for change allowed them to become innovative and responsible and build key relationships.

When President Mandela retired in 1999, his (and our) environment changed overnight. We started his post-presidential office with a dining-room table, one computer, a fax machine, a fax line and one telephone. Our infrastructure had collapsed overnight. We didn't know what to expect from life after his presidency. When he called up Prof Jakes Gerwel the next morning to ask him to organise a plane to take him to a remote area, Prof told him in a joking manner that he no longer worked for Madiba and that we didn't have access to private aeroplanes anymore. He had to travel by commercial plane. For me, this season of change was the hardest time of my professional career. But somehow, we managed. You simply do. Despite all the frustrations and challenges, we tend to come out stronger on the other side.

Change becomes more challenging as you grow older. You're set in your ways, and you want predictability and the assurance that you won't be confronted with situations that you're not prepared for emotionally. As a result, older people need so much more care, compassion and understanding whenever change is introduced. This was also true of Madiba. He wanted the assurance of stability around him, and I saw the once-composed leader become agitated by change, both physically and emotionally. If his beloved wife, Graça Machel, or I were not close by, he became restless. As there was still so much to see to, I tried to get extra hands to help by appointing more staff, but they became superfluous as he soon reverted to calling me. He also began to spend more time at his home in Qunu. It seemed to offer him a sense of stability. Having navigated so much change in his life and adapted to a range of circumstances most people wouldn't be called upon to contemplate in their lifetime, being back in his childhood territory completed the circle for him and brought him peace.

PART III

Interpreting Madiba's legacy

A rmed conflict is not new to humanity. Nor is the once-in-a-generation emergence of singular men and women who try to resolve such conflict. But in a world where opposing forces have the power to literally wipe humanity off the face of the earth, the need for leadership is more critical than ever.

I've often been asked what I think Madiba's views would have been on Russia's invasion of Ukraine on 24 February 2022. Naturally, his legacy is open to interpretation, but it's also open to misinterpretation. It's true that Madiba felt indebted to the Soviet Union for its support of the anti-apartheid movement, and he expressed his gratitude on several occasions. He held President Mikhail Gorbachev in high esteem for bringing an end to the Soviet Union, and he generally had a good working relationship with Gorbachev's successor, Boris Yeltsin. Madiba's last state visit before he retired was to Russia, but that does not mean he would have approved of Russia acting with impunity against a now sovereign state. (Until the dissolution of the Soviet Union in 1991, Ukraine had been one of the republics that made up the union.)

When a US–UK coalition invaded Iraq in the early 2000s, Madiba made a strong public pronouncement to the leaders, President George W Bush and Prime Minister Tony Blair, to condemn their invasion of an independent country. My guess is that he would have said the same about Russia invading Ukraine.

I repeatedly remind myself that there are multiple sides to the leadership and character of Nelson Mandela. It would be a grave mistake to focus on only one aspect. But one of his strengths was an ability to break down or simplify matters so that everyone understood his goal and vision – and it inspired people to follow.

Even during this war in Ukraine, where the right side and the wrong side seem clear-cut, there are complexities. Like most of the world, I've been baffled by South Africa's foreign policy on the war. The government claims it's taking a neutral stance but has abstained from voting on United Nations resolutions condemning the war.

To make sense of it, I've tried to break down the complexities to a simple analogy too. If your friend saves your life, you're indebted to them. That's similar to the Soviet Union helping the liberation struggle during apartheid. However, if your friend then commits a serious crime, such as murder – provoked or not – surely you can no longer stand by that person, who is now a criminal? Blind loyalty has far-reaching consequences, and as we've seen in the ongoing war in Ukraine, it's added a layer to the battle between superpowers who have been fuelling the war.

The South African government's response to Russia's invasion of Ukraine is like allowing your friend to act with impunity. When it comes to value-based leadership, the world should know what you stand for. Surely we can't stand by Russia indefinitely while they invade independent countries just because the Soviet Union, of which Russia was a part, helped to save our country some 30 years ago?

When you talk about the degeneration of the moral fibre of society – specifically in leadership and self-development – the inability to stand by principles highlights a lack of values and morals. Every head of state and government across the world is being tested in leadership, and their principles are being exposed through their condemnation or approval of the war. It's a true test of leadership – one that's tragically turning out to be a spectacular failure. And South Africa is dismally failing at it, too. It takes vision and courage to lead in conflict, even when you're not directly involved. It's also true that while condemnation for

Russia's actions is necessary, we should continue to drive an agenda of peaceful resolution through negotiations as our President has been doing.

When Madiba was facilitating the Burundi peace negotiations, his approach was one of inclusivity and dialogue. Having experienced success through negotiation in South Africa, he recognised the importance of bringing all stakeholders – even minority parties – to the table so that everyone would feel that they had a voice in the peace process. To this end, he had meetings with, among others, civil society, religious leaders and broad-based interest groups.

His starting point was to build trust and confidence between the various parties – similar to what he did in South Africa. He recognised that trust had been eroded between the Hutus, Tutsis and Twa in Burundi as a result of the 1993–2005 civil war, and he required all parties to acknowledge that. The deep-seated animosity was justified, but through frank and open discussions he worked towards getting all parties to buy into the vision of reconciliation and healing. For him, building trust was the foundation of a peaceful settlement.

He encouraged them to act with integrity, live up to their promises and show respect – even to those they felt did not deserve it. The social reforms that were put forward – similar to the Reconstruction and Development Programme during the first few years of South Africa's democracy – would first acknowledge that inequality was part of the divide between people, and second, provide the promise of a better life for all.

As we know, an accord was signed by all parties in Burundi to pave the way for a transitional government with power shared between the Hutus, Tutsis and Twa. Much to my frustration, the long-winded meetings lasted for days. But knowing that so many lives were saved as a result of the patience and resilience of the negotiators and all the parties involved made it worthwhile.

To Madiba, any one life mattered. Today that doesn't appear to be the norm for many politicians. The value of a life has decreased because our own respect for life is withering. I sometimes find myself thinking that either side in a conflict deserves whatever's coming to them. And then I remind myself that having these thoughts means I can't claim to value life. If you truly value life, you won't argue for retribution but rather do whatever's in your power to save even just one life. That's the kind of leaders we need today. Not people who side with any party, but rather people who advocate for peace no matter which side they're on. As we witness the abhorrent leadership of those involved in conflicts around the world, we can hardly assume that we're being led by men and women who truly value life.

In 1999, a group of influential Jewish businesspeople and academics from the US urged Madiba to enter the fray in the Middle East to try to pave a way for peace talks in the centuries-old conflict between Israel and Palestine. I'm now often asked what his views might have been on the situation after the Hamas attack in southern Israel on 7 October 2023, when hundreds of innocent young people attending a music festival were slaughtered or taken hostage by militants.

There's no single lens that can be used to view the complex problems in the Middle East.

Although I'm absolutely clear that injuring ordinary citizens for a cause can never be justified, at the same time I can't help thinking about the harsh circumstances I witnessed in Gaza during our visit there in 1999. Palestinians were generally living in grossly undeveloped areas, with barbed wire separating progress from desolation. To see children glaring at you through fences guarded by armed soldiers leaves an imprint on your psyche that's hard to forget. It was traumatic to observe how overpopulated some areas were, as people were pushed towards the sea in their own country. My views on the current conflict are coloured by that visit and are therefore biased.

At the time, Madiba made it clear that a key requirement to resolving the conflict was that both parties accepted and acknowledged publicly the independence and existence of each state within its borders. There still was, as he pointed out, the need for an international mediator that enjoyed the trust and confidence of both parties. I'm not aware of any leader or public figure in that position. It's difficult to believe that out of eight billion people in the world, the two parties can't agree on one such person.

To address the question about what Madiba would have thought: just as he admonished the US and UK for invading Iraq in the early 2000s, I believe he would be appalled by the humanitarian crisis unfolding in Gaza as a result of these two superpowers fuelling the conflict in the region. Madiba famously said, 'we know too well that our freedom is incomplete without the freedom of the Palestinians.'

Watching the war unfold on social media is, of course, another level of living hell. And it exposes so many societal flaws. In war, all people claim righteousness. Always. But who gets to decide about the value of a life – any life? Is value measured by who you pray to? Is the age of the child that died important, or does mentioning it become a means of inflicting more pain on the enemy? What do people think the answers to these questions will justify? Both sides seem to be keeping score of the deceased. Is there a point of saturation or evenness? It's simply heartless. People post polls for and against the war, and I wonder whether the outcome will save or cost another life. Are people aware of the generational hatred that they sow through social media while commenting on these events?

Once you destroy an enemy, there'll always be a new one. The children of today will remember the pain inflicted on them and grow up to start their own movements. The death of a civilian by any means during war is inhumane, irrespective of how it's done or by whom. On both sides, people claim righteousness and superiority. But if you want to claim to be superior to others, then do better!

The fact that there's a world war brewing in 2024, despite all the resources we have at our disposal, is an indictment on all of us.

And even as we focus on the wars in Eastern Europe and the Middle East, because that's what the media feeds us, conflicts rage elsewhere too. There are also rumblings of discontent at home on the southern tip of Africa. Many young, unemployed black people are angry and accuse Madiba and his colleagues of 'selling out' – by compromising with the apartheid regime during the negotiation process and thereby avoiding a military showdown. Yet, around the world, people regard Madiba's leadership during conflict as one of the most impressive feats in modern history.

The truth is that South Africa was on a knife-edge many times before the 1994 elections. The ANC and liberation political parties were only unbanned in 1990, and the apartheid regime still wielded power right up to the first democratic elections. Today's young people can't imagine how desensitised we, as ordinary citizens, were about bomb explosions and mass killings during those years.

In 1992, the National Party (NP), headed by President FW de Klerk, received a clear mandate by the white population in South Africa to proceed with the abolition of apartheid. People generally felt that the sanctions from abroad were inhibiting growth and, even though fear and uncertainty awaited them, many felt that we had to move forward. I was one of those who voted against abolishing apartheid. Through indoctrination and propaganda fed to us on every level of society, I grew up being fearful of the ANC and the black majority.

Today, I'm the first to admit that I was wrong and apartheid served my privilege. Ironically, you'll search far and wide to find others who voted against ending apartheid. Many white people want to claim that they helped bring an end to apartheid; on the other hand, some want to be able to say they were wrong for advocating an end to apartheid. But you have to live with your conscience. And making peace with yourself, with your past, goes a long way towards measuring how much you've grown as a human being. We all find it hard to admit our mistakes, as it involves humility and soul-searching, but it's what the world needs most right now. A mistake should not be a death sentence. It encourages honesty in a society dogged by dishonesty.

What I was not aware of at the time, during the dying breaths of apartheid before the 1994 elections, was that a group of about 100 000 conservative white Afrikaner men had gathered in Potchefstroom, a town in the North West province mostly surrounded by farming communities. They were determined to derail the negotiations between the ANC, NP and others as they tried, against the odds, to carve out a way forward for our complex society. These Afrikaner men were heavily armed, and it took all of Madiba's negotiation skills to persuade them to stand down.

But ANC officials were also feeling the heat: they thought negotiations with the white minority had failed. In true Madiba fashion, he called a meeting and allowed all officials to give their input. They all argued for the armed struggle to be turned up a notch, short of declaring a full-scale war on the apartheid state. Madiba listened intently without offering his opinion. This was consistent with what he'd learnt from attending meetings of his elders while he was growing up. Later in life, he implemented the principle that a leader's purpose was always to listen and observe, and at the end, provide a summary of deliberations.

Madiba then asked two simple questions. First, he asked the officials if they knew how many weapons the apartheid government had. They nervously looked at one another. No one was able to answer.

After his question was met with silence, he put the second question to them. How many soldiers did the apartheid government have? Again, his question was met only by furtive glances and frowns all around the table.

He gave them a moment to reflect and then asked rhetorically: 'And you want to go to war?'

It was the end of the discussion, and no one raised the possibility of a bloody civil war again. Madiba wanted them to decide for themselves, based on fact, whether they were ready to go to war.

When I asked him about this and about people who yearned for war, he was clear that MK had been ill-prepared at the time and, had there been a civil war, far more liberation fighters may have died than the members of a trained, organised army that had weapons and ammunition at its disposal, along with the resources accumulated during apartheid. You cannot go to war if you don't have sufficient information about the enemy.

Apart from the odds I've already described, due to a string of politically motivated killings between the ANC and the IFP, there also wasn't a united front among black people to engage the apartheid regime in war.

Madiba was a revolutionary at heart, but he became a global icon by leaving an unforgettable impression on the world when he chose peace over conflict. He chose a future for all South Africans rather than just for a select group.

As I've already said, one of Madiba's best traits was to make people feel that they belonged. In his view, you were never inadequate. He was particularly good at creating a home for everyone. In return, people showed him similar grace throughout his life. Many of these people don't make it to the history books. Among them are two critical figures in the story of Madiba and Winnie.

Douw Steyn was introduced to Madiba in 1990 by Thabo Mbeki, who had included him in a group of prominent South African businessmen who travelled to Lusaka for talks with the ANC during the mid-1980s. Douw was among a handful of white Afrikaans businessmen who defied the rules of apartheid at a time when it was not regarded as desirable to speak to the ANC. Many years later, Douw accommodated Madiba when he left his marital home in Soweto abruptly one night after finding that Winnie had disrespected the marriage. Madiba stayed with Douw for more than six months while Barbara Masekela, his chief of staff at the ANC offices, and others tried to find alternative accommodation in Johannesburg for him and the grandchildren in his care. While Madiba was good at creating an emotional space for people so they could relate and feel safe, Douw was good at meeting the material need of a roof over his head at a critical time.

The other family that deserves a mention is the De Waals from Brandfort (now called Winnie Mandela), a dusty rural town in the Free State province in central South Africa. I met Meyer de Waal, son of Adele and Piet de Waal, in or around 2016, and he told me about an occasion when he'd met Madiba in the early 2000s. He reminded me that we had also met on this occasion when he'd brought his wife and children to greet Madiba at his house in the Cape Town suburb of Bishopscourt. When Meyer began his story, I listened with only half an ear, my thoughts hovering between 'oh, at least here's another ordinary person who got to meet Madiba amid all the allegations that I overprotected him', a completely unjustified thought.

Meyer and his daughter Jade had, on separate occasions, written to the Nelson Mandela Foundation and he produced a letter that Madiba wrote from prison in 1983 to express his gratitude to Piet and Adele for caring for Winnie while she was banished to Brandfort and placed under house arrest. In the letter, Madiba expressed the wish to one day meet and thank the De Waals personally; unfortunately they both passed away before he could do so. Meyer and Jade wanted to ask whether they, representing the De Waals, could meet Madiba. Piet had been appointed Winnie's lawyer while she was in Brandfort, and his wife, Adele, had opened their house to her. Winnie had apparently often referred to Adele as her 'white sister'. They'd spent many hours talking, and even sewing and baking, which created a safe space for Winnie away from her small, simple house in the township on the outskirts of the town. The family had cared exceptionally well for

Winnie and, after receiving Jade and Meyer's correspondence with the foundation, Madiba wanted to meet them even though by that point he and Winnie were long divorced and not on speaking terms.

It would be incorrect to assume that Madiba was not wounded by the challenges and difficulties of life during his journey of 95 years. He was an angry young man, rebellious and frustrated when he was imprisoned for the first time in 1962. But he always knew that he had righteousness on his side. It would be equally wrong to say that he was the same angry person after his release from prison in 1990. Yes, during the Convention for a Democratic South Africa (Codesa) multi-party negotiations, there were glimpses of the angry Nelson Mandela. The refusal by FW de Klerk's National Party to agree to provisions set out by the liberation parties was a matter of great contestation. Today, many of those who accuse Madiba of selling out haven't bothered to read the minutes of those meetings. But to say that he was an angry man throughout his life would be far from the truth. Anger, he believed, served no purpose.

It was precisely because he was able to move on from his anger, rather than allow it to dictate his life, that he created a new life with Mrs Machel during his sunset years. If we spend too much time thinking about our anger, it infiltrates our everyday life. It's like a dark cloud hanging over your head, and it can be a cause of depression.

Many critical things have been said about Mrs Machel, but whenever the subject has come up, she's always been quick to remind me that you'll find people who dislike you everywhere in the world. It's not unique to any one person's life. No one is completely and wholly loved by all.

When you enter her house in Mozambique's capital, Maputo, the first thing you see is a beautiful picture of her deceased husband Samora Machel next to one of Madiba. Like Madiba, he was the liberator of his country and someone who will be etched in history as one of the greats. People often comment critically about the picture occupying such a prominent position in the Machel house, where Madiba had to face it every day when he spent time there. But this assumes Madiba was someone who was petty and jealous, which shows a lack of understanding of who he really was. A deeper understanding of the situation is required, not to absolve Mrs Machel but to put history in perspective for both sides.

The way I see it is that for many people, there's one big love of their life – the person that they feel 'completes' them. For Nelson Mandela, that was Winnie Madikizela, and for Graça Simbine that was Samora Machel. But fate and circumstance had different plans for both couples.

During Madiba's 27-year absence, Winnie became someone he didn't know, and Samora's tragic death altered the storyline for the Machels. Then Madiba and Mrs Machel, devastated for different reasons, found companionship, happiness and love with each other. That doesn't mean that they stepped into the shoes of the other's former spouse. Both Winnie and Samora were very present in their lives, regardless of their absence, and Madiba and Mrs Machel respected what the other's former partner meant to them. It speaks of a maturity that adds to the tragedy of their respective love stories.

At the end of Madiba's life, Mrs Machel was there to hold his hand. When the specialist on duty at Madiba's bedside said 'Mum, he is gone', the first person Mrs Machel called to be with Madiba was Winnie. She got her private moment with him. The family had gathered downstairs in the house, and Mrs Machel had even invited Ruth Mompati there – a prominent ANC leader who'd had a child with Madiba in their youth. It speaks of Mrs Machel's consideration for all the women who'd loved Madiba at different stages of his life. Those who cannot see the beautiful and powerful grace that she brought to Madiba's life are tormented with childish jealousy of her role in his life. It requires a fair amount of class and understanding to show appreciation for people who loved your partner at a different time. To say that Madiba was hurt or offended by having Samora's picture in the house is therefore simply not true. In all things, including this, he showed an extraordinary ability to see all sides, and therefore also the bigger picture. His example encourages us to do the same.

PART IV

Hope is powerful

Hope is a powerful weapon, and [one] no one power on earth can deprive you of.

– *Nelson Mandela by Himself: The Authorised Book of Quotations*, p 115

I've often wondered how it's humanly possible to remain hopeful for 27 years in prison, an achievement even more remarkable when the actual sentence was life imprisonment. I guess you'd have to grieve the loss of life as you knew it. But do you ever accept your reality? Is it even possible? After arriving on Robben Island, Madiba and the other political prisoners set about negotiating with the authorities for better living conditions. This in itself was a sign of hope, of being determined to make the best of the circumstances.

At first, only white and Indian prisoners were issued with long trousers as part of their prison uniform, while the rest got shorts – in the middle of a Cape winter, during the rainy season. After a long process of writing letters to prison authorities to point out the unfair discrimination, Madiba himself was offered a pair of long trousers. But he rejected them, saying that unless the privilege was extended to all prisoners, he wouldn't accept them. Every other week, the political prisoners – jailed for defending their principles – addressed another issue. Sometimes a privilege was granted; often it was denied. Yet, they never stopped trying. Their resilience in the face of adversity teaches us the importance of perseverance and determination in pursuit of our goals. Every choice we make becomes part of the goal we want to attain.

As for the reason they were there: evidence from documents seized at Liliesleaf Farm in the Johannesburg suburb of Rivonia implied that they were planning to overthrow the government. The farm was a secret location where members of the ANC's fledgling MK met, but the project detailed in the documents was never launched and, although acts of sabotage occurred, there was no evidence, no witnesses and no proof that Madiba was ever responsible for any violent crimes. Today, white conservatives eagerly share a fake document about alleged bomb blasts ascribed to Nelson Mandela. These claims are false, fabricated to discredit his legacy. Perhaps to those conservatives the claims seem more plausible than a life sentence for being implicated in an abandoned campaign. But that was the reality of apartheid.

Among those incarcerated with Madiba was his close friend Walter Sisulu, who was a source of inspiration and taught his fellow inmates that no matter what the situation, they had to be determined to triumph in the end. To survive, they had to focus on their hopes, not their fears, and on what brought them together as individuals – not what might drive them apart. The same powerful message applies to us today. Indeed, in my daily life, I try to draw on the lessons and wisdom I gained from Madiba to guide my actions and interpretation of events. Only in this way can his lessons become a living legacy.

By 2017, Zuma's presidency had become untenable. In addition to the accusations of corruption, an accumulation of political blunders was affecting the country's economic stability. Many South Africans had had enough. In April that year, large crowds took to the streets in major city centres and even in small towns to call for the president's removal from office.

I joined a march from Church Square in Pretoria to the Union Buildings and later a rally in Cape Town where we marched to Parliament. I was apprehensive at first, expecting people to express their anger at me over the Twitter drama. But there was none. People had moved on, and now I was singing and toyi-toying with people from all political orientations and walks of life. There was camaraderie irrespective of your political beliefs, background or origin. Of course, Zuma branded the protests as racist. But by 13 February 2018, pressure from the public had mounted to the extent that the ANC recalled Zuma and, on Valentine's Day, he publicly resigned.

How we had underestimated our collective power, I thought. Yet it was something Madiba had believed in and practised every day. It was an example to me of how, when we put aside our differences and align towards a common goal, so much can be achieved – in terms of facilitating change in our circumstances and in the way we relate to others. Sadly, the norm is for us to seek out in our friends and acquaintances people who think and feel more or less the same as us.

With digital advertising, you're fed what you're interested in. If, for example, you click on a link to look at a particular car, you'll keep seeing more advertisements for that brand and for similar cars. Algorithms and AI do the same with political interest. Once you've researched a particular stance, you'll be fed news and advertisements reflecting your views, which will only serve to strengthen them. And this is not limited to the internet. It's called an echo chamber, referring to the constant affirmation of your established thoughts and feelings, which has the effect of reinforcing them. It contributes to our intolerance of other people's views.

There's hardly a figure on South Africa's political stage who provokes a stronger response, from supporters and opponents alike, than the astute Julius Malema. I was on a commercial flight from Johannesburg to Cape Town one day when I noticed that he was on the same flight. As I no longer moved in political circles, we hadn't bumped into each other for some time. Julius is a master at playing up populism, and he often offends and irks the white Afrikaner community with his pronouncements. He unnecessarily agitates, always playing to the crowd. He's perceived as a 'white hater' because, among other things, he's been advocating for land redistribution without compensation, and fear of the possible consequences gets some people so worked up that they don't carefully look at the situation or the person as a whole. You simply have to separate politics from the person. Politics are toxic, and the internet latches on to our insecurities. Our Constitution provides for land redistribution, and only in the absence of a willing-buyer/willing-seller agreement can land be redistributed without compensation. The ANC's failure to implement its own policy has led to the issue becoming a burning one no matter the validity of the facts involved.

I was hoping to see Julius as we disembarked from the plane to thank him for reaching out to me during the Twitter war. There was nothing else to be said about it, but I was touched by his gesture. As I walked to the luggage collection point, I found a large group of mainly white people surrounding him, offering high fives and taking selfies with him. I simply smiled and walked past, thinking how people loved to hate a public figure because it was fashionable – but without ever considering the facts around an issue. Then, when they saw the person in public, they quickly forgot why they'd professed to hate him so much.

I was also pleased to think not everyone had bought into the propaganda Julius so richly spread, and at the same time I wondered how many of the bystanders had, at some stage, had a go at him for his pronouncements. One can only hope that people will continue to believe that we can triumph over our fears by stepping outside the restrictions of our own thoughts and feelings. Julius remains an important role player in South African politics irrespective of people's personal feelings about him. He, like any other person, deserves my respect because he showed me humanity in a time of crisis.

In the new South Africa, one of Madiba's main tasks was to convey to the white population that being hopeful about the future was in their interests. People were leaving the country out of fear of what the new dispensation would bring. Whites expected retribution for years of oppression. He appealed to even the hardened Afrikaner nationalists by using symbolism close to their hearts: he wore the Springbok rugby jersey and cap at the 1995 World Cup final at Ellis Park stadium in Johannesburg. By showing his association with the team, he gave them something to be hopeful about. Above all, he demonstrated that it was possible for integration to happen without people giving up their identities.

South Africa reached three more World Cup finals: one in 2007, another in Japan in 2019 and the most recent in 2023 in Paris, France. By then, the majority of South Africans were loyal supporters of the national rugby team. When the 2019 final came round, I chose to watch both the semifinals and final alone, knowing that I wouldn't be able to control my emotions in public. A few days before the final, South Africa's largest online news site asked me to write a letter to Madiba, as I usually did on key anniversaries. Here are extracts from what I wrote:

We are struggling to keep the flame of hope burning, but you taught us that even in the direst of situations, there is always a glimpse of hope.

The past four years have been tough – politically, financially, socially. And on the sports field, it has been no different . . . I've tried my best to remind people about your view that such is the nature of sport. Sometimes you win and sometimes you lose. How you conduct yourself during the game is more important.

Referring specifically to the World Cup, I wrote:

Sport has the power to unite people like no other event . . . But we cannot expect to win if we secretly believe we are incapable or undeserving of the title, as you warned.

Khulu, this is a watershed moment for us again. Symbolically, Siya [Kolisi, the captain] has taken the baton from you. He represents what we want to be as a nation – a humble, simple, authentic unifier . . . you showed us that sometimes it is important to set your differences aside and make a leap when an opportunity like this presents itself to become psychologically stronger as a nation, in our individual efforts to achieve a healthier nation. We need a paradigm shift just for encouragement and to recalibrate, and this could be it . . .

South Africa won the Rugby World Cup for the first time since Madiba's passing in 2013, but the win was not as important as the hope and inspiration it instilled in all our citizens. For a moment, we forgot about the challenges that face us. I was one of the many armchair coaches and selectors in the run up to and during the world cup. In my view, Handré Pollard was simply not the best fly-half we had. After Handré's impeccable performance during the final when he converted six penalty kicks, I realised that I had been completely wrong. Even though I had not shared my views in public, I obtained Handré's number and sent him a message, congratulating him. I said that I was one of those who had not believed in him, and even though he did not know about it, for that I was sorry.

Few occasions can move people to act like sport can. It felt as if this time we'd done it on our own, without Madiba. It restored our confidence in our own ability to achieve great things if we worked together as a nation. This is critical to remember as South Africa charts new territory with the Government of National Unity being established after the 2024 national elections. We can achieve anything if we work together to create a better life for all South Africans.

In trying to understand how they managed to survive in prison, I asked Madiba about being with people you would probably not have befriended outside. Imagine being locked up with your colleagues for 27 years, or with people from your community WhatsApp groups! There will always be those we don't get along with. It's simply down to difference in personalities. That was the case with the Robben Islanders too.

When I asked about getting on with all the different characters, Madiba said they had to accept the fact that they were 'there for life'. To make the situation bearable, you had to be self-aware and comprehend that you had characteristics that others may not like. You had to assess yourself first before you started picking at aspects of others you didn't like. Once you'd accepted that your stay on the island would be lengthy, you had to think of the survival of both your body and mind. You had to recognise that every person there came from a different background with different life experience. He said it was therefore wise to try to extract as much knowledge from others, and draw on their experiences, whether you liked them or not.

You also knew that everyone had strengths and weaknesses, and you had to focus on the strengths rather than extract the weaknesses. What you focused on would become the basis for a relationship.

One can look at the group in Block B on Robben Island as men of impeccable character. They never gave up on the world they had envisaged for all of us.

I often find myself in conversations where people bemoan the situation in South Africa. Many of their sentiments are justified. But if you constantly listen to negativity, it becomes contagious. I then always think of Madiba.

During Covid-19, I did a podcast about my thoughts on lockdown and the insights we could take from Madiba's incarceration about remaining hopeful. The main points were:

- Get up every morning with a positive mindset. If Madiba and his comrades had decided at any point that they were losing the fight and should give up, they would never have achieved freedom. Again, his leadership was on full display: being hopeful is a choice.
- Take time to contemplate. Madiba often said that he missed prison. I quickly told him that wasn't something he should say in public. But he explained that he hardly had time anymore to sit and think about problems. When you take time to contemplate, even just by putting down your mobile phone and taking five minutes to view a problem from all sides, solutions often become clear.
- Draw strength from the knowledge and experience of those around you. We've all had different experiences in life, and our particular

skill sets may not always seem helpful to us but could be the answer for someone else. Listening to understand, and taking time to discuss problems and challenges, creates new possibilities. Another point Madiba raised was how much enjoyment he got in prison from listening to those around him, drawing on their experiences and arming himself with new ideas and solutions.

- Remain clear and committed about the end goal. Throughout his imprisonment, Madiba didn't fight for his own freedom as a priority; the struggle was about freeing all people from oppression. He was clear that his freedom would be pointless unless *all* his people were afforded freedom, dignity and equality.
- Read and study. Reading in prison gave Madiba and others the opportunity to travel outside the limitations of their imprisonment. Books transport you to far-off places, allow you to share in others' experiences and broaden your horizons. Consuming social media is not reading. We need to read novels and biographies to help us see beyond our frustrations and circumstances, which often blind us.
- Have gratitude. I believe that gratitude creates fortitude. When you speak to people in rural areas of South Africa, people who have never known anything but the struggle to survive every day, they'll always tell you they're grateful for something. Throughout his imprisonment, Madiba remained grateful for his colleagues, for life and for his intellect. In the letters in *Conversations with Myself,* his gratitude for experience, kindness, friends and family shines through.

From these points, we can look at our own situation. We want bearable lives. Hope often seems to evade us. Among other things, endless hours of loadshedding at times and poor service delivery across the country frustrate us. It's unacceptable, and we should be angry, but let's channel our anger into action that uplifts and strengthens.

I wish I could have asked Madiba about social media, for his thoughts on how people sometimes push others' buttons and bring out the worst in them. It's hard to imagine what he would have made of our world with social media in it, although they must have had a non-tech version of it in prison – talking to and about others and experiencing the flaws of those around them daily. As many journalists can attest, while Madiba was alive, when they had written critical articles about him, he would invite them to breakfast to discuss their differences in opinion. It is therefore hard to imagine that he would have ignored social-media criticism if social media were part of his life.

Madiba always protected other people's dignity. At worst, he would say, 'Oh, that one will give you trouble,' or 'He is a difficult person,' but he would never attack someone's character or speak disrespectfully of them. Highly evolved people never ponder the flaws of others but rather focus on the positive things they can take from their experiences. He was adamant that if you believed the best of everyone around you, that is what they would deliver.

To be inspirational requires that we remain hopeful even during the most challenging circumstances when conditions have become a breeding ground for hostility. Instead of looking for inspiration from outside, we need to find it within ourselves.

When I travel abroad, I frequently come across teary-eyed expats telling me how much they miss South Africa. They emigrated for opportunities and what they believe to be a better life, and I won't judge them for it. But they miss home and profess that life in South Africa was generally better than where they are now. There's a lesson in that for us all. Don't get me wrong: I sometimes have to pull myself away from social media because the negativity infects me, too. But then I think of Madiba in prison and how the hope he held on to certainly did not come from outside. So, I tell myself that now is not the time to lose hope. If he could remain hopeful *every single day* for 27 years, what's *your* excuse?

Our country isn't what so many had dreamt of when they cast their democratic vote 30 years ago, and it's easy to forget what we've survived as a nation. It's also easy to get sucked into engaging in the blame game. I'm reminded of what Madiba often said to me, using words similar to these quoted in *Nelson Mandela by Himself*: 'It has been easy to blame all of our troubles on a faceless system: the Crown; the church; hierarchy; globalisation; multinational corporations; the apartheid state. It is not a hard task to place blame. But we must look within ourselves, become responsible and provide fresh solutions if we ever want to do more than complain, or make excuses.'

The fall of apartheid was a long, tedious process, like unravelling a million pieces of twisted string. International pressure, through sanctions, the armed struggle, defiance and protest, all contributed to its demise. It was a slow process of intent, not an onslaught followed by a fight that shifted power from one side to the other.

At the height of apartheid, when Madiba was still incarcerated on Robben Island – South Africa's version of Alcatraz, where political prisoners were sent to be forgotten about and to die – he spent his time wisely and, like the pragmatist that he was, with intent. Not being allowed to write regular letters to his family, loved ones and colleagues, he used the time to write to prison authorities and argue for better living conditions. I smile thinking how it must have irritated the authorities to receive a letter from the person they'd hoped would be silenced by imprisonment.

Putting pen to paper creates a paper trail, which will then become undisputed fact – something he must have known from his legal training. Writing it down also elevates the level of seriousness, as it creates a document for discussion and sets out your intentions and requests on paper. There was always a firm, serious tone to the letters he wrote, but they were also courteous and respectful, even when they contained threats.

I also witnessed this during the writing process for *Dare not Linger: The Presidential Years*, the follow-up to *Long Walk to Freedom*. I would often clear weeks in his schedule to allow him time to write. We would travel to Shambala, Douw Steyn's game farm in the north of South Africa, where he had built Madiba a house where he could enjoy privacy, peace and quiet.

As soon as we arrived, Madiba would start writing in all earnest. He'd write a few pages and hand them to me to type up. When I'd finished, I'd hand them back to him and he would start making changes. Soon he would give me a new, neatly written version of those pages. It was a tedious process, but every word was written with intent.

When I helped him remove his shoes and placed them next to his chair, he'd ask me to put them neatly facing the same way, with the toe ends exactly in line. It frustrated me because I sometimes felt that he would have taken a ruler and aligned them perfectly if he could. But like everything else in his life, this was done with intent. When he did his exercises in the morning, every movement was with conviction. Every word he spoke and action he executed was in line with who he was as a person. For him to be a leader who inspired people, small acts mattered. There was no sloppiness in his life. He had a clear purpose to bring about the society he dreamt of, and every action he performed, no matter how small or unimportant, was a stepping stone to the end goal.

You may well ask what the placement of his shoes had to do with bringing about a better society. A mindset of doing everything with consistency allowed him to be a better leader. He embodied his principles and demonstrated integrity, honesty and humility in his leadership, and he lived his life in accordance with those values. You were never confused about what he stood for. He didn't say one thing and do another. He led by example in every aspect of his life after his release from prison. He lived his life by conviction, not convenience.

It's not easy living with the same level of commitment to everything, but if you focus on small actions, your bigger ideal becomes clear. It just takes discipline. If, for example, you consider yourself anti-racist, you won't allow small situations in which racism is perpetrated to slip by around you.

Once, a friend relayed a story to me that was told by a farmer, and in his retelling he repeated the farmer's derogatory language. He tried to mask the words with the excuse, 'You know that's how old farmers talk.' I was extremely upset about the use of the language, but more disappointed in myself that I hadn't pointed out that it was unacceptable, no matter who'd used the word. I also didn't appreciate the generalisation. I've always believed that no grouping, company, government, political party or organisation is ever just good or bad. And the same goes for farmers. Not all farmers speak in derogatory terms, and by not speaking out on the matter, I'd perpetuated the generalisation. I later made a point of bringing up the subject again. It was not well received. No one likes a wise-ass, and it was the end of our friendship. I was greatly hurt, and I had to walk away from the friendship as I felt that my values and principles had been compromised. It's not the only instance where I've ghosted people and learnt to move on without fanfare. I cannot bear the use of derogatory language. If you live with intent, you're not a bystander in situations like these. You speak out against every injustice. The people who have done this have changed the course of history – people who have lived with intent to change the status quo. In doing so, there's no need to be cruel and vindictive. It can be done gracefully without any party feeling that they've been humiliated.

The problem is that social media creates a very one-sided approach when it comes to dealing with conflict. After my bruising Twitter experience, I've watched how other people were treated – as if we were back in an age where public execution was the norm. Let me state clearly that there can be no justification for racism, sexism or misogyny. But once the storm has passed, I wonder whether the 'perpetrator' has learnt anything from the experience. The shock of the wave of abuse is likely to overshadow *why* it was unleashed, and the learning gets lost in the trauma. Sometimes the intention is only to cancel and to shame, not to teach. Often it's to gain popularity for bringing someone down. I wonder if contacting the person and discussing their comment to explain why it's not acceptable might have a bigger impact.

Drawing on my own experience, if I'd discussed matters with like-minded people, they would have pointed out to me where I risked erring. We can't read intent on social media, but the worst comment in circumstances of shame usually gets the most retweets, likes and follows. Bringing others down to gain popularity is not the intent we should live by. We should take people with us on a journey and teach by sharing our experience and knowledge. That requires patience and compassion.

And, when you're the one who has to be brought into line, are you open to receiving advice from someone when they tell you your comments can be perceived as derogatory? Or do you believe you're always right? Are you ready to add an 'if' or a 'but' to justify racism or any other type of derogatory comment?

Madiba befriended his prison warders to understand how the Afrikaners thought. He learnt our language because he knew that if he wanted to negotiate with the regime, he had to understand the people in charge. He won them over in many instances, and even the hardened authoritarian types paid attention to his every word. He spoke to the Afrikaners' hearts in their language and skilfully brought people around to hearing his side. The lesson is that we have to speak to absolutely everybody.

Self-care and doing what is good for you are high on the agenda in the world today. I've learnt to appreciate how important self-awareness and mindfulness are to self-development. These two concepts are often used interchangeably, but they're different in focus and application. While self-awareness is the ability to recognise and understand your own feelings, thoughts and behaviours, mindfulness is to be present and fully engaged in the moment, without distraction or judgement.

If I look at Madiba's example, his self-awareness was key to his emotional intelligence, which underpinned his ability to recognise and manage his own emotions while taking into account those of others. I've referred to our first meeting, which was extremely emotional for me. I was in shock because the person in front of me had an exhilarating aura about him, and in that moment, self-reflection became almost unbearable. I broke down in tears as I lost control of my emotions. He thought he'd caused it, but the baggage of the past that came sharply into view in that moment was the real cause. He deliberately didn't let go of my hand and, in a stern way, told me to compose myself but with a smile on his face. Over the years, I've seen thousands of people across the world react like I did. Others have been apprehensive when meeting him. His total commitment to seeing and seeking only the best in others holds up a mirror to our own lives. He knew that people admired him for being able to forgive without harbouring resentment. Because it requires such discipline and self-respect, we find it difficult to imagine how this is humanly possible.

His every interaction created a special moment, for he reflected only the best in all of us. He showed us who and what we could all be, because he was not a god or a saint but a man with vices and virtues, like all of us. By being mindful about himself, he demonstrated what was possible if you became aware of how your presence affected others.

With his staff, he always insisted that he did not want to inconvenience anyone with his presence. When crowds overwhelmed him and his bodyguards had to shield him, the guards were not allowed to be rude to members of the public. When we were driving in peak-hour traffic, he didn't want to delay other road users because 'we are *all* in a hurry', he would say.

Being mindful requires you to be humble. But humility doesn't imply that you have to be weak. In fact, my first lesson from Madiba in

1994 was about being courageous, standing up for myself and learning to say no without sounding conceited.

When Madiba took FW de Klerk on a fundraising drive for their respective political parties, he made sure that he was always the one who introduced De Klerk with words of warmth so that everyone could relax and understand that the approach was legitimate and equal and that they harboured no resentment towards each other. Although they were competing for funding, Madiba wanted things to be fair. By humbling himself, he showed the guests that he was, in fact, the more senior in status of the two men. There was no need to humiliate De Klerk; Madiba believed humiliating anyone would reflect more on himself than on the other person.

And, when it came to acknowledging a mistake, he did not shy away because he understood that apologising did not require you to sacrifice self-worth. The simple words 'I am sorry, I was wrong' are hardly ever spoken these days. Everyone is competing for righteousness and popularity, and we think being wrong in any situation makes us look weak and sets us back in our quest for success.

Madiba could be stubborn, but he was never unmovable. When he made it known that he wanted to reduce the voter age to fourteen before the 1994 general elections, a cartoonist drew a baby in a nappy, pacifier in the mouth, casting its vote. That cartoon convinced Madiba that fourteen-year-olds were too young for the responsibility, and he accepted it with humility. It was one of the strengths of his leadership style that he appreciated complexity and nuance – human beings were sometimes wrong and sometimes right. In today's world, we make up our minds about people based only on what we see on social media. Yet, Madiba himself was complex: he could be stubborn but kind and strict but compassionate, all at once.

When we're wrong, we often feel that we need to justify ourselves, while in fact saying, 'Sorry, I was wrong,' is sufficient. It removes the sting from the situation if we simply admit our mistake. Often explaining reverses the gains made by an apology – anything after the word 'but' negates it. 'I am sorry I was racist, but I was antagonised' simply means that your ego is too big to accept that you are wrong and that racism is wrong. To be willing to be corrected requires you to be humble and self-aware. This implies having a healthy self-esteem and self-confidence: you're aware of your accomplishments, strengths and weaknesses, and you feel confident in your ability to take risks and pursue your goals. Ultimately, most people want personal growth, and self-awareness helps you to understand the areas in your life that need improvement and the steps to take to address them.

I've learnt that being aware of the implications of your actions and words is important for effective communication. When you're aware of your own emotions and habitual reactions, you can manage them better in challenging situations. This prevents conflict and misunderstandings, and being able to say how you feel about things helps you steer clear of the pitfalls of creating situations of conflict. In some cases, simply avoiding a situation in which I know I'll react in a certain way is the wisest way to avoid conflict.

Whenever you met Madiba, he made you feel like the most important person alive. As mentioned before, he was in touch with himself and could manage his own emotions and behaviour. With mindfulness, he was able to engage any person he met without distraction.

In a face-to-face conversation, how often will someone start checking their mobile phone, look past you at something else or lose their train of thought because they're distracted? Being mindful requires one to be fully present in such interactions. When friends visit, I find it difficult to attend to anyone or anything else. It's probably age-related and a function of my curiosity that I don't want to miss anything: I want the person in front of me to have my full attention. Whether Madiba was interacting with a vagrant or a CEO, he didn't appreciate being distracted or interrupted by someone else. You would then see his forceful personality emerge, a harshness he never otherwise showed.

He despised disrespect, and paying attention to the person in front of him without interference was his way of respecting others. In the age of instant gratification, we find it difficult to focus on one person at a time.

If you're mindful in a conversation, it reduces stress and anxiety because brain scatter is minimised. Two of my friends have taught me to cross my fingers when I'm reminded of something while someone else is speaking and I feel the urge to interject. I can't write this off as an age problem only because both of these friends are not yet 40. We now cross our fingers to remind us to wait until the other person has finished their story before making our contribution. It's really effective in facilitating meaningful conversations. I also tend to listen better when I stop myself from interrupting others. I assume the best approach to mindfulness in social media exchanges would simply be not to type immediately.

It may have been helpful that Madiba never had a mobile phone, but I doubt that anything would have distracted him or made him less present in his engagements with people. When the first mobile network company in South Africa began to operate, Madiba posed with a mobile phone in hand to introduce the new technology to the public. Yes, he was an influencer back in the day! But the phone was soon discarded, as it was not something he wanted to learn to manage. He didn't grow up with technology, and his absence from the world for 27 years had prevented him from embracing the progress. There was a car phone installed in his official vehicle, but he would never switch it off after ending a call. In his mind, when you put down the receiver, the call was terminated. I think he also secretly enjoyed the silence or listening to the radio rather than people disturbing him while he was being driven around, and eventually the phone had to be removed from the car as it created complications for everyone.

One of Madiba's great strengths was his ability to connect with people irrespective of their ideology, class, status, background, religion or appearance. He made every person feel special in that moment because he was present, mindful and self-aware.

Practising forgiveness also requires mindfulness. Madiba is hailed across the world for his ability to forgive his oppressors – the people who imprisoned him and denied him the best years of his life. I've alluded to how forgiving his oppressors not only freed him of constant hatred and resentment but also freed the oppressors of the burden of self-hatred. In doing so, he made us all stand tall despite our history. To him, it was a burden we all shared and, being mindful that living with guilt eats away at you, he knew that denying his oppressors forgiveness was cruel and unnecessary. When you forgive, it doesn't mean you must have a relationship with the person who harmed you. But you need to let go, and that only happens with forgiveness.

I have mentioned how Madiba had the opportunity for self-reflection while in prison. We ought to take time every day to reflect on what we did and said, and to think about our problems and challenges. I do this before I go to sleep every night, and I often think of a word in an email that could be misinterpreted. I sleep on it, and if I feel in the morning that I wasn't attentive enough, I contact the person to explain. I'm not second-guessing myself but being mindful of how my actions and interactions are perceived by others.

When New Zealand Prime Minister Jacinda Ardern resigned from her position, she said, 'I hope I leave New Zealanders with a belief that you can be kind but strong, empathetic but decisive, optimistic but focused. And that you can be your own kind of leader – one who knows when it's time to go.'

Whatever the criticism against her, these words reminded me so much of Madiba's character. Women are expected to be strong, but not too strong because then you are perceived to be arrogant. You're told to protect yourself but not too much because then you're seen to be difficult.

During a recent conversation, someone mentioned an older woman who had never married and said, 'You know how difficult older single woman are.' I was quick to say, 'No, I don't know how we are, tell me.' Whether you're alone by choice or circumstance, people don't realise how much you need to fend for yourself as a single, middle-aged woman. Nothing happens without a fight. You fight the injustices of sexism on all levels every day. But then you're considered impossible, rude or unreasonable when you stand your ground.

These tags and labels become easier to bear as we get older. I no longer care whether I'm being called arrogant or difficult because, ultimately, I have to protect myself and my sanity. I've learnt that I'm not a crowd animal. I hate conforming with the prescribed rules of 'how women should act'; sadly, too many men still want to dictate to women what they should think and feel.

The most respected and influential woman in South Africa is not intimidated by men, their status or their threats, sexism or misogyny. She never raises her voice and beats the argument with facts and a softer approach every time. Advocate Thuli Madonsela reminds me a lot of Madiba. Her demeanour, how she addresses people, her steadfast principles and her humility and respect, even to her enemies – all without sacrificing her self-worth – are admirable.

As Madiba said in *Nelson Mandela by Himself*, 'we accord persons dignity by assuming that they are good, that they share the human qualities we ascribe to ourselves'. In the modern world, people find it difficult to imagine that enemies can respect one another. Yet, throughout his life, Madiba perfected the art of using respect as a personal and political tool to win over his enemies, disarm his opponents and diffuse difficult situations.

A core part of his character was the desire to attain equality through the symbolism of respect. He created an environment in which people communicated as equals. What his legacy teaches us is to choose humanity over blind ideology. You don't have to respect all beliefs, ideologies, convictions and traditions, but you have to respect the right of anyone to hold a belief, conviction or ideology.

At first, I had trouble adapting to this. I tended to hold on to resentment, especially when someone had been cruel without justification. In South Africa, especially as a result of social media, people have forgotten how to 'disagree without being violently disagreeable', as US civil rights leader Martin Luther King Jnr said. Madiba led through living by authentic example. He showed us that we could respect the opposition, an enemy or a foe, even those who had harmed us, and that it was not a reflection on their character but on ours when we chose to respect those who were least deserving of our respect.

On our journeys through the world, I saw how people reacted when they met Madiba. It was a brief moment during which they could interact with the world's most loved leader. He was always approachable, extending his hand and ready to be touched by his admirers – although it was a great cause of concern for his security and staff.

To the world, Madiba was an enigma. He inspired resonance and unity, and when you met him in person, he acknowledged your complexities as a human being yet treated everyone as an equal. No one felt patronised; even if he lowered himself to your level, it was not in a condescending manner. When he made small talk, he looked you in the eyes, infecting you with that beautiful, generous smile, his face receptive to your emotions and your need to be recognised as a mere mortal aspiring to greatness. He appealed to your kinder instinct because that is what he radiated with such generosity.

As I've said, you always knew exactly where you stood with Madiba on any matter because of the way he conducted himself. He was consistent in his beliefs and habits, and you never had to guess how he felt about a particular issue. He wasn't punctual only at times. He was *always* punctual because it was a matter of respect. On many occasions, he would simply cancel meetings or dismiss people when they were late because of tardiness and a lack of respect. You can't be an effective leader if you're not punctual and you don't inspire others to be respectful of your time. When the organisers of an event were not ready to start the programme at the scheduled time, it didn't deter Madiba from going on stage and simply continuing with the proceedings.

In July 1995, with the eyes of the world upon us as we emerged from being a pariah state, the South African Rugby Union (SARU), largely run by white Afrikaner men, produced a top-class rugby world tournament. SARU president Dr Louis Luyt stood alongside President Nelson Mandela when the national anthem was sung and accompanied him onto the field after the Springboks received the Webb Ellis Cup.

A year later, Madiba established a commission of inquiry to investigate suspected nepotism and racism within South African rugby. Dr Luyt contested the president's decision and considered it an overreach for him to interfere in matters concerning a private sports body. In preparation for the court case, Madiba's counsel argued that he should not go to court as the opposition would try to humiliate him. They insisted that his legal team would appear on his behalf and defend his decision. President Mandela, however, insisted that he wanted to go to court. As it had been his decision to establish the commission of inquiry, he wanted the opportunity to defend that decision. His eagerness to appear in court was clearly not imitated by some of his successors.

I was embarrassed on behalf of Dr Luyt, who had basked in Madiba's limelight during the World Cup and was now challenging the authority of the president in a court of law. Rugby is what it is in this country today because of Madiba. It was a sport supported by the minority in South Africa, but, through his actions, it became a sport embraced by everyone. Imagine the scenario if he hadn't walked out onto the field that day in 1995. Imagine if he'd appeared but in his own clothes. How different would our history and that of rugby have been? And now SA Rugby was meeting him in court.

That morning, in the car with Madiba on our way there, I made my disapproval of Dr Luyt's actions clear. The president looked pensive throughout the short journey from his official residence to the court in Pretoria. We entered the Pretoria High Court, a stuffy building with low ceilings. As was customary, the people in court all rose as the president entered. Madiba walked straight up to Dr Luyt's counsel and extended his hand. Silence descended in the courtroom, and the atmosphere was thick with tension. 'Goeiemôre, hoe gaan dit? [Good morning, how are you?]' Madiba asked Dr Luyt's all-white Afrikaans team. I could see the surprise on the senior counsels' faces. In their minds, there was supposed to be anger and animosity between the opposing sides in a court battle.

By this time, I'd become a fierce supporter of Madiba. It had taken me time to reconcile with my past and work through the anger of being misled by apartheid propaganda for years. Nelson Mandela and the ANC's fight for equality, humanity and dignity for all people in South Africa were principles with which I now identified.

I wanted to interrupt when Madiba reached out to greet those lawyers, but it was uncalled for in that moment. The mere proximity of Dr Luyt made me uncomfortable. He was a big man, and his posture was somewhat intimidating. President Mandela looked small beside him, although Madiba himself was just inches short of six feet, lean and muscular. I hovered around the back of the courtroom, hoping to avoid making eye contact with Dr Luyt, who knew me as one of Mr Mandela's secretaries.

In situations like these, President Mandela always made a point of introducing his entire delegation to whoever he was dealing with. But luckily for me, he didn't that day.

During the tea break later that morning, I confronted Madiba and asked: 'Mr President, did you realise that you greeted Dr Luyt's lawyers – the people who have the audacity to challenge your authority despite everything you did for them – before you greeted your own?'

He looked at me with surprise and invited me to sit down. The room was dark and stuffy, with the windows closed for security reasons. He started off by explaining that the nature of law required two sides to appear before a judge to separate fact from fiction, weigh the legalities on both sides and decide on a way forward. He said that a court case was therefore not a battlefield, and one would be wrong to assume that the function of the court of law was for personal battles and feelings. I kind of knew this but had never thought about it in detail. I'd been taught that courts were used to threaten people and intimidate the other side, while in fact that was not the purpose of the law.

By greeting Dr Luyt's lawyers first, Madiba wanted to show them that it was not a personal battle but a matter before the law. First, he said, 'You never allow the enemy to determine the grounds for battle.' By greeting them, he showed them that it was purely a legal and not a personal battle. Second, he said, 'The way you approach a person will determine how that person treats you.' By being courteous and reaching out to people who are supposedly aggrieved by your actions, you diffuse a situation. By respecting the opposition, they have no choice but to treat you with respect because you've disarmed them. His lesson in respect was meaningful far beyond the courtroom.

In 1999, Madiba set out to campaign for the ANC for the national elections, after which he would retire from public office. As the elections approached, we set out on the campaign trail, criss-crossing the country to convey the ANC's message of a brighter future for people in South Africa and to build on the legacy of his presidency. As Madiba appealed to the coloured community more than the incumbent, Thabo Mbeki, it was felt that he would have more success campaigning on the Cape Flats, the suburbs on the outskirts of Cape Town where coloured people lived.

When we arrived, we walked the streets of Mitchells Plain, where people were relaxing after a week of hard work. South Africa has a terrible history of what is referred to as the 'dop system'. Mainly coloured labourers on wine farms in the Western Cape were paid with wine and a little food to top up their meagre wages. This created a dependency on alcohol that has left a legacy of abuse and violence in coloured communities even though the dop system has been declared unlawful and employees are expected to be paid a minimum wage. The president's visit to the area did not discourage people from enjoying their Saturday afternoon; it was only mid-afternoon, but some residents were already tipsy.

I noticed one woman standing in the doorway of her house – a small, semi-permanent one-bedroom structure with rocks on the tin roof to secure it during storms in the windy Cape. The reception Madiba received in Mitchells Plain was lukewarm. A few curious bystanders followed the president's entourage, and generally people moved to the pavement to get a better look as he passed by. Yet this woman stood in her doorway unmoved by the commotion. Her face was emotionless as the president waved at her.

He stopped and walked to the doorway. 'Middag [Good afternoon],' he said to her in Afrikaans, the language spoken by most coloured people in the Cape. She just nodded. We became uncomfortable, as it was unheard of for someone not to respond to the president's friendly greeting. 'Kan ek inkom [May I enter]?' he asked. She looked surprised and not quite sure whether she was ready to receive him. It was clear from her assertiveness that her political conviction weighed heavily on the decision whether to allow him inside or not. 'Ek kan sien jy is kwaad [I can see you're angry],' he said. She may not have been angry, but the fact that he acknowledged her emotions relaxed her a little. He immediately followed with, 'Hoe gaan dit [How are you]?' without giving her time to contemplate whether she was angry or not. When he extended his hand, she took it. Probably intimidated by his closeness, she took a step back even though she was now holding his hand. He moved towards her, and they entered her house.

He invited himself to sit in her simple lounge while making small talk to settle the atmosphere. The security staff remained outside, and I stood in the doorway. A few ANC councillors had followed him into the house and were now sitting or standing around him, crowding the small room. He said, jokingly, that he was thirsty, and she offered him tea. She was nervous but realised that the moment would probably be more bearable if she kept herself busy by boiling some water.

The president then started asking about community issues that affected her: safety, service delivery, employment. A brief interaction followed, during which he mainly listened. He offered few solutions to her complaints but looked at the councillors with every point she ticked off her list. Then he simply said, 'I have heard your complaints, and we will look into these matters. We are trying to establish an organisation that cares for all people in South Africa equally. I understand your frustrations and I hope that my colleagues here will attend to these issues speedily. They are men and women of integrity and when I give them a task, they always fulfil it.'

The woman felt heard. It was so typical of Madiba: always willing to listen and acknowledge people's existence. There was no blaming the councillors for the failure to deliver what the woman expected from the government, but his expression of trust in their ability to resolve the issues appealed to their better selves. His confidence in people encouraged and inspired them to live up to his expectations.

Whether they would fulfil the promise to the woman we wouldn't know. Madiba finished his tea and got up to leave. As we walked out of the woman's yard, we saw that a large crowd of people had gathered outside. People were curious to know why the president had visited this woman's house. Possibly they were a bit jealous. Whether you were a supporter or not, the fact that a sitting president had entered your yard elevated your status. The woman remained in the doorway. It was quiet for a moment as we walked out, and then she exclaimed: 'Jy weet, ek het nog altyd gesê hy's nie 'n swarte nie, hy's 'n coloured

[You know, I've always said he's not a black, he's a coloured]' – to much laughter from the crowd. Madiba ignored the comment, but as he bowed his head and kept walking, a smile tweaked the corners of his mouth. Then his face broke into a huge grin. Nelson Mandela was a black man, proud and vocal about his African identity and heritage, but paying attention to the woman and going into her house so that she could be heard had made him so relatable to her that she wanted to claim his identity.

On our numerous business visits abroad, we never had time for sightseeing. When I'm asked about our travels, people always ask which country I liked most. It's not something I can answer, as our visits were limited to state guest houses, palaces and hotels. I can offer advice on the best hotels in the world, but sadly I don't have much information about the touristy side of any country.

Shortly after Madiba's retirement, we travelled to Saudi Arabia to raise funds for the establishment of the Nelson Mandela Foundation. We'd planned a tour to a few countries for Madiba to plead the case of the foundation to various heads of state, governments, business leaders and friends. Having just left office, Madiba was enjoying a new level of freedom to do what he wanted instead of what he had to. The private plane that was due to fly us to Europe was only scheduled to collect us from Riyadh a day after we'd finished our meetings, and when I asked Madiba what he wanted to do with that time, he surprisingly announced that he would like to visit Mecca, the holy city millions of Muslims travel to annually to take part in the pilgrimage.

The Saudi government had offered to provide logistics for any plans Madiba may have had while in their country, so I hastily started the arrangements. As I was the only official travelling with Madiba – apart from his medical doctor and security contingent – the Saudi protocol officers had no choice but to engage with me, a woman, about the arrangements.

When they returned in the early evening to ask some more questions, I said, 'What time do we leave for Mecca tomorrow morning?' The men looked at each other and switched over to speaking Arabic. I stood there for a few minutes trying to gauge by their body language whether there was a problem and if I could expect an answer soon.

The leader of the team looked at me with embarrassment and said, 'Unfortunately, Madam, you cannot go to Mecca, only President Mandela will go.' I explained that he would not go unless I went with him. (He would not travel without me, as he relied on me for guidance and communicating his needs.) I'd already been with him to see the king, who'd shaken my hand, something that was unheard of in Muslim culture, and I couldn't see why they wouldn't allow me to travel to Mecca with him if I'd visited the king already. Again, they started conversing in Arabic and, seemingly having decided to come clean, the senior official said, 'You cannot travel to Mecca because you are not a Muslim.' You could have knocked me over with a feather. Without thinking, I said, 'But President Mandela is not a Muslim either.' They resorted to Arabic again, and I could sense that I'd caused a slight panic. 'Wait a minute, wait a minute,' they said and left for their office. They returned an hour later and sympathetically conveyed that Mr Mandela would not be able to travel to Mecca because he too was not a Muslim.

I was dumbstruck. The Saudis are probably some of the most hospitable people you'll find in the world. When it came to Madiba, no expense was spared to ensure his comfort and enjoyment while in their country – the best cars and the most comfortable hotel. Even when dinner was served, it was in excess. I was puzzled by this for a long time. There was nothing Madiba had done, and nothing in his behaviour or mannerisms, that could have made them believe he was Muslim.

It was only after I connected the visit to the coloured community and the visit to Saudi Arabia that I realised that it was precisely his ability to respect people's cultures, traditions and beliefs that made them claim him. His relatability to people made him so revered because he could connect to the human being in front of him regardless of religion, ideology, traditions or culture. Whether he was surrounded by royalty or people of stature, class or wealth, his character remained intact and his respect for people – irrespective of the differences that set us apart – remained steadfast even in the most daunting of situations.

I believe that people are inherently good, yet we battle with good versus evil daily. We are creatures of contradiction. To be released from prison after 27 years, show no resentment and carry no desire for vengeance is something that is unfathomable to most of us. It's precisely that battle within ourselves, the weakness of our humanity, to which Madiba appealed. He acknowledged our vulnerability as human beings and showed us that if he could overcome his vulnerability, so could we.

I cannot be Madiba. In fact, anyone who even tries will find it hard to imitate his consistency. But he still lives in my heart and mind every day, and whenever I go to a shop or use a service where I'm attended to by a waiter or an assistant, I make a point of looking the person in the eye, acknowledging them with a smile and finding something positive to say to them – whether it be a compliment or simply something relating to our interaction. When they wear a name badge, I make a point of repeating their name and finding some personal connection with it. My interaction with that person can be just another mindless moment of functionality, or it can leave them with a thought or a feeling. It may be the only compliment that they receive that day, or they may be going through something too complex and painful to share in our brief interaction. So, I am aware of every word and the feeling that I'll leave with that person when I walk away. I engage fully, trying to be present. I'm sometimes distracted by my phone while unpacking my groceries at the supermarket till, and then I deliberately pull myself back into the moment because not looking the cashier in the eye and greeting them with a brief word is, in fact, demeaning to them. During my public speaking engagements, I sometimes ask the audience whether they can remember the name, eye colour or clothing of the person who last served them in a shop. Very few can.

When I've made a point of engaging, I walk away feeling uplifted because I had the power to show that person that they didn't have to buy into the single story of what I represent. I gave them an opportunity to change their mind about someone. I left a flickering of hope with them that the world can be a caring place. And that is what Madiba did every single day in his interactions with people.

It would be incorrect to assume that Madiba was not prejudiced. The difference is that he was open about it, whereas most of us try to hide it for fear of being shamed. Shortly after his retirement, he was scheduled to travel from Pretoria to the Northern Cape on a small military aircraft. We were used to flying on jets, and this small plane with its exposed propellors looked flimsy and unreliable. Understandably, we were a little uneasy. As was customary before boarding the plane, we met the pilots. The captain of the aircraft was a white female officer. I think Madiba thought at first that the women he met were stewardesses because he became very quiet once he was seated and saw the two women taking their positions in the cockpit.

Throughout the journey, he kept leaning out of his seat to look down the aisle to the cockpit to see whether they had the plane under control. He hardly said a word during the flight. The journey was uneventful and comfortable, but his uneasiness was noticeable. When we arrived at our destination, Madiba disembarked and again greeted the pilots as he usually did. Smiling, he said to the captain, 'You know, I have never been flown by a female pilot before, and I must tell you that I was very nervous. But you did such a good job that I really hope to be flown by you again in future.' The women burst out laughing and took it as a compliment, oblivious to the personal dilemma he'd faced.

Former Springbok wing Bryan Habana recently reminded me how, whenever they met, Madiba would ask him about Cape Town. Madiba assumed that because Bryan is coloured he originated from the Cape, like the majority of coloured people. We corrected Madiba on a few occasions, reminding him that Bryan was actually born and educated in Johannesburg, but he would often slip back to the association very innocently, allowing his preconception to dictate.

In his early life, Madiba commented that the ANC's defiance campaign was 'much more successful in the Eastern Cape where there were no Indians'. He later realised how insensitive his comment had been and, during the drafting of the Freedom Charter in 1955, pressed hard for co-operation between all racial groups, including minorities like the Indians and Afrikaners.

I admired Madiba for being able to recognise and admit his prejudice. In a similar vein, I was amazed when a white friend who had adopted a black child told me, 'I battle my racial bias every single day.' It was a powerful yet sobering confession. Thinking about it later, I realised we simply don't know what we don't know. To admit to your blind spots is something few people do. Trust me, my friend excels in bringing up that child, and he in turn is an unbelievably generous and kind-spirited human who is teaching his parents in return as they work through their feelings and experiences on this complex journey. What both my friend and I have concluded is that we all battle our racial bias and prejudice every day, and admitting it is like a moment when you cross the Rubicon. The realisation that you should not be afraid to acknowledge your struggles is crucial in dealing with them.

Amid the rise of social media and cancel culture, few people can express their feelings today for fear of being shamed. Therefore, we don't deal with our prejudices and biases. We hide it so no one sees our vulnerabilities; it takes a person of character to deal with their prejudice and bias in public.

In certain cases, it's sufficient to admit that you don't know enough about something to have an opinion on it. It's more impactful to express your lack of knowledge about something than to force your views and opinions on others. Just as I need to take responsibility for being sensitive to how my choice of words affects others, it's important for similar consideration to be exercised by those who are trying to raise public awareness. You can be a feminist, LGBTQIA+ advocate or campaigner for any cause without alienating and offending precisely the people you wish to influence. The term 'woke' refers to being enlightened and multiculturally sensitive. But for me, wokeness has taken on a different meaning. I do consider myself multiculturally sensitive, sometimes perhaps not enough, but people have exploited these sensitivities to force certain behaviour – and I have a problem with that. What the experience of indoctrination during apartheid has taught me is that I will not allow anyone to force their views, beliefs or traditions on me, and I've become acutely sensitive to not doing it from my side either.

From watching Madiba, it was clear to me that a leader should create the space for people to speak freely, confidently and openly about the things they struggle with. Being open about his own blind spots allowed others to be vulnerable without fear. Social media is doing the opposite, and problems like racism are being swept under the carpet. Some people like to point out that they are colour-blind. In my view, unless you're visually impaired, none of us is colour-blind. The question should be, what do we do with the differences we observe in each other? Do we let them define how we act or treat someone?

I've touched on growing our awareness of and sensitivity around language and the words we use. It's my hope that we, individually, will also grow in maturity so that we realise there's no need to get defensive when someone points out that a particular term – even though it may have been used for centuries – is now considered offensive. For example, referring to someone as a nanny, the help or a maid is derogatory, while carer, homemaker, housekeeper or child minder is more acceptable. It's not about being politically correct; it's about showing respect to people. There's no forum that informs us when there's a shift in the perception of certain words, actions and mannerisms, resulting in some people or groups finding them offensive. For instance, unless you're exposed to a variety of cultures and traditions, and a range of different experiences, you won't know that it's derogatory not only to the individual but also to black people in general to refer to someone as the 'black sheep' of the family. As a white person, it's hard to imagine how it must feel if you're black and the term 'black sheep' is used to describe the outcast or worst-performing family member.

I try my best to listen and to respect other people's feelings, but I've also made a fair number of mistakes and used language loosely without thinking of the unintended consequence. During one of Oprah Winfrey's first visits to South Africa, she and her entourage arrived at our offices in a van, or people carrier. I walked to the passenger window where the bodyguard was seated and said something like, 'Would you people like to get out here or wait for the van to be parked?' I can't remember the exact words or context, but I referred to the passengers as 'you people'. Oprah was offended – and rightfully so. In Afrikaans, we would use 'julle' (the collective of you) to address people, but using 'you people' in English is highly offensive. I apologised, and it was explained to her that it was because of my Afrikaans background that I had referred to the group collectively in that way without thinking of the implications.

I would like to think that I am a sensitive, changed person, but I guess that's never true about anyone. Yet it is the intent and consistency with which we try to be different and better people that matters most. What I've come to learn about myself is how intensively I despise cruelty of any kind, even when it's aimed at a common enemy.

I often quote Madiba: 'No one is born hating another because of the colour of their skin, their background or religion. People learn to hate, and if they can learn to hate, they can be taught to love, for love comes more naturally to the human spirit than its opposite.' People are not born racists. They become racists through behaviour. It's within everyone's power to unlearn prejudice, bias and racism. I often look at racist incidents and think that for centuries we, as white people, professed to be the superior race, yet there's nothing superior to being disrespectful to anyone.

The law of nature dictates that we defend the 'grouping' that we're part of. When a white person is attacked on social media, people of the same grouping will often side with the one being attacked, irrespective of whether they're right or wrong. We all try to defend our own, and there's nothing wrong with it when it's justified. But freeing yourself from the limitations of such thoughts and shifting your mind to rather seek fairness, justice and equality, irrespective of who's involved, can be sobering.

I was standing in the post office in Pretoria one day to renew a car licence. It was a hot day, and the queue was long. When there were about six people in front of me, it was the turn of an elderly black man, but he'd completed the wrong form and was directed to a table where he could sit and complete the correct form. Due to loadshedding, the air conditioning in the building wasn't working and most people were irritated at having to wait in the small room without any ventilation. The queue moved, and there were now only four people in front of me. When the old man with his grey hair and beard stood up and shuffled to the front of the queue to ask whether he had completed the form correctly, the white man in front of me exploded. 'You can't push in front of the line! You need to go to the back.' The old man turned around and said apologetically that he'd merely wanted to ask a question, upon which the man said, 'That's typical of you people.' This occurred in about 2018, many years after my incident with Oprah.

When we do something ourselves, we often don't understand why others are so upset with us until we see our own actions reflected in someone else. Then we see how cruel and sometimes irrational our behaviour was. The fight then turned white-on-white when a brave white elderly lady started defending the black man. In that moment, I also realised that I was merely a bystander. My fear of getting involved prevented me from standing up for what was right. As this event unfolded in front of me, I saw just how degrading racism was – not only to the person on the receiving end but also to the perpetrator.

You're the only person in control of your emotions. Every connection you make matters. When you lose control of your emotions, you give away your power. I thought about this incident for a long time and wondered what the old black man's general view of white people was. How did that one incident affect him? Did he know that not all white people were so impatient with others? In that moment, it must have seemed improbable to him that asking a simple question could have escalated that quickly into a race war. Where was the grace of being kind and considerate?

People can confuse being respectful with being submissive. But respect doesn't require you to give up anything. Respect should be given from a place of strength, not weakness. I ponder how much self-respect Madiba must have had to also respect his oppressors and his political opponents. By listening to people's concerns and finding common ground, he built bridges between communities and promoted reconciliation and forgiveness.

Earlier in this book, I referred to how Jacob Zuma and his carefully created Bell Pottinger strategy had divided people by blaming apartheid to mask fraud and large-scale corruption. Thirty years later, we can't use apartheid as an excuse for poor governance. However, there's a difference between blaming your own shortcomings or criminal activity on apartheid and recognising the pain of apartheid. Many people can't bring themselves to acknowledge the pain that the system caused. They tell people blatantly to move on from apartheid, or they claim to have apologised, yet they won't accept the pain the system caused. How can we not accept that discrimination is immoral? We live with a litany of inconsistencies and ask ourselves why our nation cannot heal. And if you're standing around the braai, the subtle racism continues. We perpetuate what we tolerate, and no real change can be effected unless we insist on respect for all people, even in their absence.

Madiba's impact on my life has changed the way I think and feel about many things. It's difficult to quantify or measure, but I've tried by being honest about my beginnings in order for me to measure my ongoing change. Hopefully, by confronting myself I'll encourage others to soften their hearts and reconcile with themselves and the past.

Madiba is still present in my everyday life. I'm sometimes accused of idolising him and am often told to stop referring to him. 'We are tired of your stories with Mandela,' someone once sneered at me on social media. I've also heard comments such as 'Do you have nothing else to talk about than Madiba?' Our frame of reference in life is our experience. If I see a date, for instance 2004, I immediately think where we were and what big things happened with Madiba in that year. Oh, it's the year he 'retired from retirement', as he said, I think to myself. If I'm expected to erase my memories of him to accommodate others' feelings, I would expect others to do the same. It's simply not possible for anyone to erase nineteen years from their life.

I continue to share my recollections of the person I knew because I believe that part of repaying the enormous privilege I had of working for Madiba is to keep telling his stories and reminding the public of his legacy. His presence in my life remains an immeasurable gift, and I intend to share that gift with others for as long as I can.

It's an exceptional privilege to be one of only a few people to have known Madiba so intimately and to have witnessed his remarkable achievements first-hand. Fifty years from now, none of us will be around. Maybe even sooner. But for now, we should tell our stories and solidify the beautiful legacy that he left behind.

The Mandela legacy organisations – the Nelson Mandela Children's Fund, the Nelson Mandela Foundation and the Mandela Rhodes Foundation – have all moved on and are creating their own identities shaped by the modern world. They give new impetus to his belief in humanity and the world through the work they do.

I, too, have moved on, and life has taken its twists and turns. I now live in the Cape in a small coastal village away from the hustle and bustle of the city. It's a place where people greet each other every morning. I'm happy here, but I sorely miss the energy and diversity of the north. After nineteen years of extreme pressure and stress, I had to find solace and serenity. Also, remaining in the same place for too long makes you lose touch with the longitudes and latitudes. It all blurs together, and you no longer pay attention to the sum of the small parts that make up life.

In Gauteng, I would find myself on the road for an entire day, driving from one appointment to the next, exhausted by the end of it all, but having achieved nothing but engagement in social activities. It was something I could not sustain. I'm not a complete hermit, but I now have a place to hide. I value time by myself more than ever and love being close to nature, where I experience so much beauty every day. I'm no longer consumed with politics, and I have moved away from meaningless actions and relationships that don't serve any purpose but instead exhaust me emotionally (I put a lot of emotional investment into all my interactions). I've learnt to rather adopt a measured approach, and I am exactly where I'm supposed to be at this point in my life.

When people find me living in a small town, they ask, 'Have you retired?' I have *not*, and can*not*, retire. I still enjoy my work engage-ments, meeting people and sharing my life journey with others, in addition to the charitable organisations I support. But I do, however, have the luxury to choose how I spend my time. Life is but the wink of an eye, and I value every single day, by the grace of God.

My two beloved Boston terriers, Winston and Indira, also passed away, but then I got a second chance at love with my two French bulldogs, Che and Eva (named after Che Guevara and Eva Perón). I have healed, and sometimes I feel as if I've finally grown up, even though I still struggle with many interpersonal issues. I have priorities, and I'm clear about what I value in life in terms of morals, values and principles. I miss Madiba, but I speak about him regularly when I leave my sanctuary for my motivational speaking appointments.

I've struggled to write this book because it required me to open wounds that I'd hoped could be buried beneath the scars we all carry. Madiba reminded me many times that if you didn't face your problems head-on, they would always be with you – and, in writing, I have had to relive and heal from many things. He taught us all to carry our scars with grace.

I've learnt that Beyoncé doesn't look at all the replies on her social media posts, which is certainly the best thing anyone can do for their own sanity. I've learnt to curb the urge to see or hear what others think or feel about me. It's unhealthy seeking validation from people you'll never know.

Importantly, I've been reminded that if you remain quiet in the face of injustice, you contribute to the society we despise for its cruelty and unfairness. Madiba taught me to stand up and speak out, and I will neglect my covenant to him if I remain quiet about injustice around me. But he also taught me a kindness and compassion that I did not know before. It's been a foundation for meaningful interactions with people from all walks of life, which is something that no academic qualification, thesis or other life experience could have taught me. On many occasions, I may have blurred the lines or confused standing up for something with the worthless need just to say something, but I've grown so much in the process and continue to do so.

Kindness is always the strongest force and can disarm any situation that is tense. Love and laughter, fear and pain, and hope and acknowledgement are universal currencies, and to use them to bring people together is what we should take from Madiba's life.

In the mid-2000s, whenever Madiba visited Shambala Private Game Reserve, I drove along the N1 highway from Pretoria to Polokwane. At one stage, the roadworks to rebuild the national highway, which took months to complete, caused huge delays. I was happy when they had completed the bulk of the work and I could drive uninterrupted to the farm. One hot February afternoon, I noticed a group of black men clearing the shoulder of the road. The heat outside was excruciating, and I became aware of the luxury of the cold air in my car. There was little shade outside, with only a few trees in the distance beyond the fence. I decided to stop, as I wondered whether the men had water to drink. I thought they would surely die of heat stroke if they didn't. Alongside the group, I saw a heap of plastic bottles tucked under a bush to shade them from the direct sunlight.

As I brought the car to a standstill, one of the men approached. I switched off the ignition and got out. 'Hello,' the man said, a smile teasing at the corners of his mouth, although he was probably too afraid to smile as it may have come across as intimidating to this white woman standing next to her car. We were still so suspicious of each other, I thought to myself.

'Can I help you?' he said. I sensed that he'd detached himself from the group working behind him to create a barrier between me and them, signifying that I would be safe speaking to him alone.

'No, I don't need any help, thank you,' I responded as I walked to the back of my car. I could see that he was waiting for me to open the boot, perhaps to remove something. He looked puzzled by my inaction.

'You know,' I began, 'I've driven this road on many occasions, and I've been so frustrated with the roadworks. Today I'm driving it for the first time uninterrupted, and when I saw you working here, I realised that it's because of you that I can drive on this road in such luxury – a smooth surface and a beautiful, clean new road.' The man stood frozen, his face expressionless.

'I thought to myself, does anyone ever thank you for the work you do?' A deep frown appeared on his forehead, not because of the question but perhaps because of its stupidity. I paused for a response but he said nothing, so I continued, 'I know you get paid; I get paid for my job too, but I get thanked by people every day and I was wondering if anyone ever thanked you.' Now the expression on his face indicated that, in his opinion, I was certifiable.

You're told never to stop along a road, especially as a woman travelling alone. Add to that our country's history and the inherent distrust between people, and many a white person would tell me that I was crazy to stop for no good reason next to a group of black men.

'I thought I ought to stop and thank you because I want you to know that some of us notice your hard work. I notice the circumstances you work under and in this heat, while I just drive along in my air-conditioned car without giving it a second thought.' Still no reaction.

I moved to his side to face his colleagues and waved at them to call them closer. He also waved at them to step closer, probably thinking, 'I must show you this crazy white woman.' I repeated what I'd told him earlier and said I merely wanted to thank them. They accepted my gesture with humility, and I said goodbye and got back into the car.

In my rear-view mirror, I could see their heads shaking in disbelief as they returned to their posts.

As I drove off, I felt as if my heart was being ripped from my chest. Those men, all middle-aged, will probably never do less menial work. Because of apartheid, they were not exposed to education or a world beyond their own suffering and survival. When their child is sick at home, they don't get to rush home to take the child to the doctor.

When their parent dies, they probably don't have the means to arrange a dignified burial. Have we truly travelled long enough in someone else's footsteps to understand what they've endured?

Not once during that interaction did I mention Madiba's name or that I was working for him at the time. As the miles passed on my way to him, I felt a deep sense of gratitude and a growing self-worth. I knew that those men would never forget the crazy white woman who once stopped to thank them, and I knew that my simple gesture would go a long way towards showing them that people could change. It's within anyone's power to change another person's life. Just like the young woman in the visa queue changed my life, I'm able to change another person's perceptions through simple actions when I show respect, compassion and empathy.

Despite our suspicion and mistrust, our prejudices and biases, we can choose humanity. South Africans are probably the most resilient nation on earth. We've overcome great tragedy and challenges, and as long as we have open and honest discussions and realise that nothing is ever lost, we'll find a way forward.

I've come to realise that the greatest gift Madiba bestowed on each of us was his ability to respect people, and in doing so he created a sense of belonging for all of us. Those with courage and enough self-respect will bridge the chasm, reach out to the other side and say, 'I care.' You may be consistently right about someone, until one day you're wrong. The opposite is also true. Let us not slaughter each other with words and judgement because we're seeking self-righteousness.

In November 2012, Prof Jakes Gerwel's wife, Phoebe, called me. 'Zelda, jy moet kom, hy vra vir jou. [Zelda, you must come, he is asking for you.]' He was a highly educated man and a 'man of the people' in the truest sense. To me, he was a father figure. Despite all his qualifications and decorations, he never dismissed people, no matter who they were or what they'd done.

I arranged to travel to the Cape immediately. Prof was unconscious when I got there, but I had my time with him. When I greeted Phoebe and their daughter, Jesse, on my way out, they explained that he'd been drifting in and out of consciousness the previous few days before his condition had deteriorated overnight. He'd been confused and weak, but the last intelligible sentence he'd muttered was, 'Julle moet in vrede saamleef [You must live in peace].'

I'm an Afrikaans white South African committed to the future of this country and all our people. I can't control anyone, but I can control myself, my feelings and my thoughts. I acknowledge and appreciate the complexities of our society and hope to exercise caution, compassion and understanding in dealing with the challenges that affect us all. I will stand up in the face of injustice and adapt to the ever-changing political landscape, just like Madiba did. I will live by principle and purpose, rather than convenience.

Along my journey, I've come to understand peace differently: it's not only peace with others but peace with the self, too – peace even with your worst mistakes. If you keep being blinded by the pain of your mistakes, you won't recognise the gift you've received. When faced with complex problems, we're often tempted to look for complicated solutions while the simplest of answers may be best.

A while ago, I bumped into Kweku Mandela, one of Madiba's grandchildren, while our cars were being serviced at the same dealership. He'd always been warm and courteous to me and treated me with the utmost dignity and respect, despite having had to overcome any differences pertaining to Madiba's life. We spoke about politics, the future and the past, and I had another opportunity to say how much I appreciated him. I'll never forget his kind embrace at Madiba's funeral. I have a small replica statue of Madiba that I cherish, which Kweku had arranged for me years ago after businesspeople had donated the life-size statue to our offices. On special occasions, I place a candle next to my little statue and take time to think of Madiba.

He carried the flame of hope and encouraged us all to do the same. He made us belong by forgiving us, loving us and inviting us to join hands and overcome the challenges we face.

He famously said that he hoped our choices would always reflect our hopes, not our fears. In 2004, at the 10th anniversary of our democracy, he said: 'My wish is that South Africans never give up on the belief in goodness, that they cherish that faith in human beings as a cornerstone of our democracy.'

Thirty years into democracy, our country continues to evolve. We have much to be hopeful for, but we must keep challenging ourselves to do better, to acknowledge our mistakes, to work together to find solutions and to defy the odds, yet again. While the government forges our political future, we as ordinary people must find that which unites us rather than that which divides us. We must focus on our common humanity, and our mutual caring, in the spirit of ubuntu. Let us remain hopeful as we continue on our shared journey. Each of us has the power to change ourselves and our collective future.

Whenever we feel entrapped, cornered or challenged in any way, like I did early that morning at Heathrow Airport, blinded by anger, let us remember what hope can achieve.

Bibliography

Bizos, G. 2007. *Odyssey to Freedom*. Random House Struik: Cape Town.

Dalai Lama and Tutu, D. with Abrams, D. 2016. *The Book of Joy*. Hutchinson: London.

Ferguson, M. 2024. *When Love Kills: The Tragic Tale of AKA and Anele*. Melinda Ferguson Books: Cape Town.

Kasrils, R. 2017. *A Simple Man: Kasrils and the Zuma Enigma*. Jacana: Johannesburg.

La Grange, Z. 2014. *Good Morning, Mr Mandela*. Penguin: London.

Mandela, N. 1994. *Long Walk to Freedom*. Little, Brown and Company: London.

Mandela, N. 2010. *Conversations with Myself*. Farrar, Straus and Giroux: New York.

Mandela, N. 2013. *Nelson Mandela by Himself: The Authorised Book of Quotations*. Pan Macmillan: Johannesburg.

Murakami, H. 2005. *Kafka on the Shore*. The Harvill Press: London.

Ronson, J. 2015. *So You've Been Publicly Shamed*. Picador: London.

Steinberg, J. 2023. *Winnie & Nelson: Portrait of a Marriage*. Jonathan Ball: Johannesburg.

Index

Acknowledgements

To my parents and family, thank you for weathering every storm with me and loving me so unconditionally.

Every friend and close associate that has accepted me and supported me, both old and new, thank you.

A special thank you to Prof Thuli Madonsela, Prof Jonathan Jansen, Prof Hlengiwe Mkhize (in memoriam), Derek Hanekom, Songezo Zibi and Prof Piet Croucamp for caring when I had lost all hope.

To the friends who helped me pick up the pieces, I have deep gratitude for your presence in my life.

Erika Oosthuysen and her entire team at NB Publishers, as well as Gillian Warren-Brown, thank you for the enthusiasm and determination with which you approached this project.

Mrs Graça Machel, Josina, Mandla, Zindzi (in memoriam) and Kweku, thank you for the love and acceptance.

To Khulu: Thank you for the gift of a life-changing experience and the honour to have been loved by you!

To every person that has touched my life, changed me, made me think, and showed me how to be a better human being and a better South African, I sincerely thank you.

About the author

Zelda la Grange worked alongside Nelson Mandela as private secretary and his closest aid for nineteen years. As one of the few privileged first-hand witnesses to his everyday life, she is deeply committed to sharing his teachings with the world. La Grange has presented TEDx talks at Oxford, Flanders and Porto, among other international stages. She was casting director for the documentary *Miracle Rising* (2013) and co-produced a six-part documentary series *A Glorious Human Achievement: Nelson Mandela* in 2018. She co-presented *Tussen Ons*, a women's television talk show, for five seasons.

La Grange strives to be an active citizen and supports several civil society groupings working to strengthen South Africa's constitutional democracy. She is also a supporter of several non-governmental and charitable organisations, and through her Zelda la Grange Foundation aims to set up a referral system in small towns for focused and specialised assistance to children in foster care.

In 2014 she published the international bestseller *Good Morning, Mr Mandela*, a memoir detailing the life-changing experience of working for Nelson Mandela. La Grange was appointed as a trustee of the Ahmed Kathrada Foundation board in 2023.